POP!

Protect Your Retirement from the Bursting of the Baby Boomer Bubble

PAUL GHEZZI

iUniverse, Inc.
New York   Bloomington

POP!
Protect Your Retirement from the Bursting of the Baby Boomer Bubble

iUniverse books may be ordered through booksellers or by contacting:

iUniverse
1663 Liberty Drive
Bloomington, IN 47403
www.iuniverse.com
1-800-Authors (1-800-288-4677)

www.boombustzoom.com

ISBN: 978-0-595-45472-3 (pbk)
ISBN: 978-0-595-48844-5 (cloth)
ISBN: 978-0-595-89784-1 (ebk)

Printed in the United States of America

iUniverse rev. date: 11/1/10

Dedicated to:

Remo,
Assunta,
Annette,
Christian,
Erica &
Alexander

Thank you for your unconditional
love, support & inspiration.

Contents

Author's Preface

I began thinking about writing this book in 2007 because I could see the financial storm clouds gathering on the horizon. In hindsight, starting my professional career in the recession of the early 1990s has given me a greater appreciation for the boom to bust cycles of capitalism. Periods of economic expansion are, inevitably, followed by periods of economic contraction. The creation of financial bubbles and the bursting of those bubbles, much to the dismay and despair of every new generation of investors, is part of our collective economic history.

The current financial crisis, and its potential impact on the baby boomer generation, is different in scope and magnitude from anything we have experienced since the Great Depression. It's different because, as of 2010, approximately ninety million North Americans are entering their retirement years. A series of financial shocks, along with the impact of an aging North American population, will have lasting consequences for the global economy but especially for the financial well-being of the baby boomers.

I have chosen to share my thoughts and ideas about this problem and the potential solutions in parable format for two distinct reasons. The first is that I have always been a fan of parable books because of their ability to share a universal message in an engaging and nonintimidating format. This is especially true for the world of personal finance and economics. The second reason was my fundamental belief that the world did not need another financial textbook. Local bookstores are filled with countless books on financial planning, economics, and business, and yet it seems that so little of that wisdom permeates into daily consciousness and daily decision making.

My intention for this book is to share some key personal financial principles to help you prosper during the coming decade, and provide a framework for how to best apply these principles to create real and positive change in your life.

The *Bursting of the Baby Boomer Bubble* is communicated through the fictional lives of Don and Mary Stewart. They represent those baby boomers who are worried about their future and are looking for answers. The story may be familiar to you because of what is taking place in your life or the life of a family member, colleague, or friend.

My hope is that, after reading this book, you will be better prepared to protect your wealth and prosper during the coming decade of financial crisis.

Paul Ghezzi, CA

Section 1

The Crisis

Prologue – The *Big Pop*!

January 2014

It's been two years since the global economy has gone bust. The combination of job losses, stock market crash, and real estate meltdown has decimated most retirement plans. Government intervention, while at first appearing to hold promise, has not been able to revive the economy in any meaningful way. While the magnitude of the current financial crisis caught most by surprise, there were several warnings along the way; very few were willing to listen.

It was only six years ago that my employer gave me the proverbial "Golden Kick" out the door as a reward for all my years of evenings and weekends away from my family. Twenty years of dedication and service gone in the blink of an eye. Funny how nothing you do in your corporate career can ever prepare you for the emotional and financial upheaval related to the downsizing of your life's work. With a mortgage, two children in university, a new dream home, and not enough in savings, the financial pressure was unbearable. On the verge of losing everything our family had worked so hard to build, a chance encounter of the most improbable kind changed everything.

Despite the current financial meltdown, my wife and I are enjoying the retirement of our dreams. Many wonder how we can be blessed with such good fortune in such tumultuous times. They ask me for the secret to our amazing financial turnaround. I have told our story so many times that it seems only logical to commit it to paper and share it with others who may wish to benefit. To this end, I have decided to relate our experiences as a series of discussions and notes, as best as I can recall them.

The Dream Is Shattered

January 2008

I slammed my hand down on the snooze button with a heavy thud. The alarm clock was still buzzing. This was my third failed attempt to stop the annoying beeping. Between the alarm clock and the smell of coffee drifting up the stairs, I grumbled out of bed. I could feel my anger swelling like a tidal wave. *How could this happen to me? How could they do this to me? Especially now, with Andrea and Alexander in university and this blasted mortgage that feels like a noose around my neck?*

"Don," Mary called out, "you are going to be late again." This was the fifth day in a row that I was going to be late getting to the office. For twenty years I was one of the first to get the coffee perking and the paper flowing. Now I could barely motivate myself to make it in before ten o'clock. "All right, I'll be right down," I yelled.

About six months ago, a rumor started to float around the office about my division being moved to Mexico. At first I laughed it off, but there were many clues that gave credence to the rumor. It started with the discreet shifting of some manufacturing production to a plant overseas and then evolved into a discernable trend. I tried to ignore the obvious, hoping that I would be spared for all my years of service and the depth of my experience. My state of denial had come to an abrupt end the week before, when an emergency meeting was called for all division heads. The bulk of the U.S. and Canadian manufacturing operations were being shifted to Mexico and Asia for various strategic reasons, and we were going to be downsized. All division heads, and their salaries and benefits, were being let go.

Mary started her career as a stockbroker in New York, but gave up her job to raise our two children. She had just recently returned to the workforce, taking a part-time position with a local bank. The pay wasn't great, but she enjoyed the team environment and the opportunity to work her way back into the corporate world.

"Don, you can't ignore this," Mary said, trying to cover up her frustration. "Losing your job was not your fault, and I don't blame you in any way. But you know we can't afford the life we have worked so hard to create with you out of work. I can pick up more hours to help out in the short term, but you need to start making plans for something else."

Mary is the planner, and I am the procrastinator. She is the saver, and I am the spender. Every relationship is pretty much like this. One saves and plans while the other dreams and spends. She wants me to plan my strategy, and I want to bury my head in the sand or my fist into a wall. Over the last few months, all of our conversations have ended up in some sort of confrontation. A financial crisis can put any relationship, no matter how strong it is, to the ultimate test.

I have always been pretty good at climbing the corporate ladder; and now that the ladder was being ripped from underneath me, I felt totally lost. "Wake up, Mary," I lashed out. "Do you think there are a bunch of companies lined up to pick up a fifty-something-year-old management executive with a six-figure income?"

"Don, we have argued about this too many times," Mary said. "Losing your job is a reality. We need to do something to make sure that we don't lose our house and our retirement savings in the process."

I glanced over to the stack of bills sitting on the kitchen table. Instantly my blood was boiling. I felt like everything I worked so hard for was a complete lie. I reached across the table to grab the bills, oblivious to my recently poured cup of coffee. The cup crashed to the floor and burst into a multitude of jagged pieces. "Brilliant, Don," I grumbled, "this is the perfect metaphor for your smashed retirement dreams."

My head was spinning. All I could think about was, *How are we going to survive this?*

Café Milano

Café Milano could be best described as a cross between a trendy coffeehouse, such as one might find in the downtown corridor, and a neatly kept used-book store. Located in the heart of Oakhill, a town that even Google Maps could miss, it looked both out of place and hopelessly charming at the same time. Where else in town could you access your e-mail from your wireless laptop while enjoying a book, such as the *Gospel of Wealth* by Andrew Carnegie, from an eclectic library?

In many ways Café Milano represented the paradox of Mike, owner, chief coffee-server, and resident librarian. Some guessed Mike was in his late forties, while others guessed early fifties. His large green eyes could instantly cut through your early morning fog. He was as comfortable talking to Erma Williams about her ailing golden retriever as he was talking to Brad Miller about his hardware business.

When Café Milano first opened, there was a lot of talk around town about how the local coffee shops were going to run the smallish gourmet café out of town. Business was slow in the early months and most stayed away, not sure about the quirky nature of the café. But soon word spread about the great coffee, worldly décor, and interesting library. It was simply a matter of time before the charm of Café Milano took root in the community.

Since Café Milano was on the other side of town, Mary and I rarely took the extra thirty minutes to drive over for a coffee. Little did we know that hidden behind the European window treatments and earthy décor of Café Milano was the discovery that would save our retirement and change our lives forever.

Acting on a Feeling

After hopelessly watching my mug shatter on the recently installed hardwood floor, I instantly felt the need for fresh air. I was feeling claustrophobic and trapped in perpetual panic due to our financial crisis. I looked over at Mary and said, "I am going to play hooky today. Let's go to Moe's for some bacon and eggs. I need some space and time to think this through."

Mary sighed, "Let's clean up first, and give me a few minutes to get ready."

Moe's was usually reserved for Saturday morning breakfasts, but I needed something to grab onto today. I couldn't muster the energy to make it into the office. I needed some space, and Mary needed some frank and honest discussion about our financial situation. I owed her that.

After cleaning up my mess, I felt an urgency to leave the house. Mary, never one to be rushed, sat in the passenger seat of our sedan looking straight ahead with a terse and focused demeanor. I knew that look, and I also knew that right now it was best for me to be quiet. I slumped into the driver's seat, turned the ignition, and started the drive to Moe's. As we left our driveway and sped away, I could not find the strength to collect myself and my thoughts. My mind was drifting, and I recalled the scene in the movie *Cast Away*, starring Tom Hanks. At the end of the movie, the character he portrays drives up to a forked intersection and is unable to proceed in any direction for a number of minutes. The intersection represents the meeting of his shattered old life and the potential beginnings of a new life. It's that precise moment when you need to let go of the past to make room for something better, but all you know is the past, so you hang on for dear life.

That's exactly how I felt at the corner of McCauley Avenue and Gore Road. Turning right on Gore would take me to Moe's. This route felt comfortable and familiar, but suddenly, old. Taking a left at McCauley would take me nowhere I could think of that was meaningful or important. Yet my instincts were screaming to hang a left. A blast of a horn from a car behind us forced me to make my decision.

"Don?" inquired Mary. "Where are you going?"

I did not reply and continued to drive in silence until I startled Mary by slamming the brakes. I noticed Café Milano out of the corner of my eye and felt compelled to pull over. I would later explain to friends that I was just following a strong hunch. But that's not entirely true. I was running from my old life, looking for something new.

After recovering from the hard braking maneuver, Mary looked at me, more surprised than angry, and asked, "Why here, Don?"

"I don't know, to be quite honest," I replied.

New York, New York

We had only been in the café a handful of times, never this early and never alone. While we had caught glimpses of Mike working in the kitchen or chatting with his patrons, we were usually served by a young staff member.

7

From this proximity there was something very familiar about Mike, but I could not fish it from my memory banks.

As we entered the café, the first patrons of the morning, we were greeted by Mike from a distance.

"Good morning, folks. Sorry I am a little late starting the day," Mike said. Mike had a slight accent that to the nonperceptive ear sounded British. I would later confirm that it was an accent he carried from his early years as a child growing up in South Africa.

"Good morning," Mary replied. "My husband decided to take a detour from our normal route and come in for a coffee. Probably a good thing, since we could both use a little less cholesterol in our diet and some quiet time." She shot a firm glance in my direction to let me know that we would also be talking openly about our finances, whether I liked it or not.

"Kind of a spur-of-the-moment idea," I said as I looked around the café, scouring my memory in vain.

"Please, have a seat," Mike said, "and I will get the coffee perking." Mike strolled behind the serving counter and turned on the orchestra of coffee machines. He moved behind the counter with a sense of ease and comfort. At the same time, there was something wrong about this man standing behind a coffee bar.

I turned to Mary, who had picked up the local paper, and asked in a quiet voice, "Does he look familiar to you, Mary?"

Mary replied with a smirk, "Sure, if you merged Bill Clinton and Gregory Peck into one package and added a great accent to boot."

"No, Michael Douglas, from the movie *Wall Street*," I whispered, leaning toward Mary.

Before I could say another word, Mary shot back with the same enthusiasm, "New York City, the summer of 1980!"

"It can't be," I replied. "That would not make any sense. Of all the places he would have ended up, Oakhill is not one of them."

"It could be him," Mary said while tugging on my shirt sleeve. "But it's hard to be sure. The guy I remember wore flashy suits, basked in the limelight of New York, and was a media junkie. If it is him, what is he doing in Oakhill?"

Mary could not contain her excitement. In the summer of 1980 we were living in New York as Mary was completing a six-month internship with an investment bank. At the time, there was a great buzz around a young financial guru who was making headline news on a regular basis. The financial guru had taken on cult status, with his dazzling good looks and amazing ability to create wealth and move the markets. After Mary had completed her transfer, we continued to follow him through the media, until one day the young financial guru simply disappeared.

"So, what can I get you folks?" asked Mike as he strolled over with his pen and order pad.

I looked over to Mary and she shot me back a look of trepidation.

What is the best way to approach him? I thought to myself. *Should I be coy, or should I be forward? Did he want his privacy protected? What the heck was he doing in Oakhill anyway? Was it really him?*

"Earth to Don," Mary said while staring nervously at the menu. "What are you having?"

"I'm not sure," I murmured.

"No problem," replied Mike, "let me give you a few more minutes."

Before I could organize my thoughts, Mary whispered into my ear, "Those eyes, Don. Those eyes are so familiar. Could it really be him?"

What is she talking about? I thought to myself. *It's simply not possible.*

Mary continued, "He's aged, better than most, but something about those eyes is timeless."

I said, trying to sound more confident than I felt, "If you think it's him, just introduce yourself and stop making a big deal about it."

Mary blurted back, "I don't know what to say."

"Well, just go ahead and approach him with your Mary directness and charm," I said. I was just as curious as Mary. Having a celebrity figure from your youth serving you coffee in your hometown is about as surreal as it gets.

Mike made his way back to our table and brushed back his hair with his right hand. I remember that very sweep of the hand when he would be interviewed, standing in front of the building he owned in the heart of New York's financial district. The only difference was the crow's-feet around the eyes, a graying of the hair, and a slightly wider waistline. Not bad for a guy who had to be in his early sixties. I was certain Mary was thinking the same thing.

Taking a chance, Mary blurted out, "I apologize if this is too forward, but you look very familiar. I know this may sound very strange, but we think we remember you from our days in New York. I think the New York media used to call you Golden Hand?"

Mike's posture stiffened, and his face turned a light shade of red. After what seemed like an eternity of uncomfortable silence, he replied quietly, "That was many years ago, and I have left that life far behind."

Mary and I looked at each other. I wanted to say something, but before I could, Mike sat in the empty chair between us. His body was rigid, and his jaw appeared clenched. He continued, "My days as Michael E. Higgins III are far behind me now. Today I am Mike Higgins, owner and chief coffee maker of Café Milano." He leaned forward with arms crossed in front of his chest. "I prefer to live my life as Mike."

"Uh, well then, hello, Mike," I said, stumbling like a child who was confessing to his mother about chipping one of her pieces of table china. "I'm Don Stewart, and this is my wife, Mary Stewart. I just want to say what an honor it is to meet you. Mary was a banker back in New York when you were front page news."

"I get the feeling that we have intruded on your privacy, and I apologize," Mary said, gazing down with her eyes and shifting in her seat.

"Well, Don and Mary, it was really just a matter of time," continued Mike. "We live in a global village, and I knew at some point I would be revisiting my days on Wall Street. I just didn't expect it to be today."

Mike paused and took a deep breath before speaking, "It would be a gesture of great kindness if you did not share this with anyone else. I am not sure many people would actually care or even be remotely interested about an aging Wall Street banker who used to enjoy the limelight; but when you gain a certain amount of privacy, you appreciate its value."

Mary and I blurted out at the same time, "Of course …"

Mary continued, "Of course, Mike, we will keep this private."

I reiterated Mary's promise, "Yes, really Mike, we don't want to jeopardize your privacy and will keep this to ourselves. You have our word."

Feeling like she had to seize the moment, Mary clasped her hands together and leaned toward Mike, "If you don't mind, I do have one small question …"

Mike's back stiffened, and he drew his breath and held it. He knew that this moment was inevitable. It's what every doctor frets about before going to a party or social reception. The most feared question, "Hey Doc, what do I do about my aching leg?" or "Can you suggest anything for my terrible migraines?" In Mike's case, it was, "What are you doing with your money these days?" Or "Where are the markets going next?"

I noticed Mike's mannerisms change immediately. His gaze narrowed, and his brow tightened up. A would-be student of body language, I sensed the intrusion of our conversation and realized that this was what Mike was hoping to avoid by leaving New York. I decided to intervene.

I cleared my throat and said, "We first read about you when we were in New York almost thirty years ago. I was a junior sales associate for the company I work for today, and Mary was wrapping up a six-month stint at an investment bank. The article was about a young financial guru who had just made a newsworthy fortune in the gold market. Not only did you get rich, but you made a lot of investors wealthy along the way."

Still no change in his posture, I thought to myself as I continued.

"We then followed your career as you correctly moved into U.S. real estate and the Japanese stock market in the 1980s, and to everyone's surprise pulled out of both markets in 1988. You shocked people with your move, and the media blasted you for your perceived blunder. You went from financial genius to fool overnight because real estate and Japanese stocks kept going up. But just less than one year later, the collapse started and investors lost billions of dollars in wealth. You were 'Golden Hand' once again."

I noticed an ever-so-slight unfurling of his brow and a loosening-up of the crossed arms. *Keep the momentum up, Don*, I thought to myself.

"Around the same time that you pulled out of real estate, you financed a major expansion of a boutique coffeehouse in Seattle. You took a small private company national and in the process created another fortune for yourself and your investors. You helped start the buzz surrounding upscale coffee shops, which are now the norm all over North America. Then one day, you just disappeared from the newspapers and gossip magazines."

Mary jumped into the conversation and said, "You seemed to have an uncanny ability to avoid financial bubbles and capture major trends. There was even a rumor that the movie *Wall Street* and the main character Gordon Gekko, played by Michael Douglas, were based on your life story."

Mike replied with a hint of a smile, "That life is a long time ago, and I am totally content running Café Milano."

Mary nodded. She smoothed her skirt over her knees and looked up at him. "It's not easy to admit this, Mike, but I'm worried about our financial future." She sighed. "Don is losing his job, and we have two kids in college. I only have a small income from a part-time job at the bank. We could be in big trouble if we don't get these issues straightened out."

I saw Mike's body relax. He leaned forward. "There's something about you that I trust … but I am not really in the business of …"

"Any advice you have would be greatly appreciated," she said.

I watched their exchange in silent admiration of Mary's tenacity. Secretly, I hoped for a get-rich-quick idea. Maybe something we could invest in or an inside tip on a hot stock. Maybe we could earn a bunch of fast money and solve our problems quickly.

Neither of us was remotely prepared for what Mike had to share.

- 3 -

The Retirement Anxiety Trap

Mike looked directly at us and said, "Like many baby boomers, you are stuck in the "retirement anxiety trap." Unless you find your way out of this trap, you are going to experience major financial losses during the coming decade. Headed toward us is the greatest financial crisis of the baby boomer generation, and very few are prepared."

Mike had our complete attention; we were hanging on his every word. Just as he was about to continue, the front door burst open, and a family of five made their way to a table adjacent to the kitchen entrance. "Hi folks, have a seat and I'll be right over," Mike said as he turned back to us.

"If you are really interested in learning about the financial crisis that is moving our way and you want to learn how to protect your retirement, come back tomorrow morning at eight o'clock sharp," Mike said. "If you are here, then I'll know that you are serious, and I will share some of my personal plans and strategies. If not, you will always be welcome here as customers and friends who share my little secret." Mike gracefully made his way to the table with the three screaming children and proceeded to take their orders.

Mary and I sat in stunned silence. *What was the crisis headed our way that Mike was so adamant about?*

Are We Going To Be Okay?

We arrived at Café Milano the next morning at 7:55. As we entered, the smell of fresh espresso beans being ground and hot milk frothing filled my nostrils and brought back memories of family trips to Italy. Those were the heady days of spending more than we earned and riding the prosperity wave that followed the recession of the early 1980s.

"You both look like you could use a shot of java this morning," Mike said as he sipped his espresso and motioned for us to join him at the serving counter.

"We got very little sleep last night," I said. "We spent most of the night asking the question 'Are we going to be okay?'"

Mike nodded and replied, "You are not alone in this regard. That is the single most pressing question that more than ninety million Baby Boomers are asking as they head into their retirement years. Much more than a question, it is a feeling of worry and fear that their retirement plans will not be able to meet their expectations and fund their lifestyle. This is what I call the retirement anxiety trap." Mike paused to finish his espresso.

Mary asked, "Can you explain that trap in more detail?"

Mike said, "It's the emotional and financial trap that most baby boomers find themselves stuck in. As they move closer to retirement, they are not at all confident that they will be able to maintain their lifestyle and financial independence. The retirement anxiety trap creates a flight or fight response. Despite their fears about their finances and quality of life in retirement, current statistics show that the majority of baby boomers continue to overspend and not save enough."

"That pretty much sums up how we are feeling these days," I said as I glanced over at Mary.

Mike moved from behind the counter to a seat by the front window of the café and motioned for us to join him. I admired the fact that he looked slim and in good physical shape. He moved like a man much younger in years.

"In 1950, the average North American, who lived to about the age of seventy-three, experienced a retirement time frame of ten years or less," Mike said. "Today, due to advances in health care and standards of living, the average age at death for males is eighty years and for females is eighty-three years. That means that an average retirement may be in excess of twenty years. The risk that you will either outlive your capital or be required to dramatically reduce your lifestyle in retirement is growing."

I started thinking about our new dream home and how much we had paid during the past two years to finance and furnish it. The assumption we made was that we would start increasing our retirement savings in the next few years. It seemed as if we were always putting this off into the future.

Mike continued, "The strategies of buying residential real estate with a large mortgage, leveraging personal assets for consumption, placing the majority of investments in the equity markets, and hoping for a positive outcome will no longer work in the coming decade. The same strategies that for the past twenty years have inflated the baby boomer bubble will result in the derailment of many retirement plans during the coming decade."

As the meeting with Mike progressed, I became more frightened and worried. I shifted in my seat, and my body felt tense and tight. "I have to admit this is not too comforting, Mike," I finally said.

"Don't worry, Don. You still have time to remedy your situation. There are no easy fixes, but there are lots of opportunities," Mike said. "Before you can fix a problem, you have to understand why the problem exists and how it relates to your current situation. Otherwise, you will simply repeat past mistakes and will never create lasting change."

Mary, always organized, was taking notes. "What was that comment about the baby boomer bubble?"

Mike replied, "The baby boomer bubble is a reference to the unprecedented rise in personal debt, real estate values, stock markets, and commodities during the past twenty years. Low interest rates, low inflation, increased personal leveraging, an increasing appetite for consumption, and the spiraling government debt have been the key ingredients for the creation of financial bubbles in both the stock market and real estate."

Mary nodded and continued taking notes.

"Why do you feel this is about to change in a bad way?" I asked, somewhat regretting the lack of sophistication of my question.

Mike replied, "Because the era of cheap money and rising asset values across the financial spectrum is coming to an end."

Fighting an annoying scratch in my throat, likely a result of my increasing anxiety, I asked Mike for a glass of water. He moved behind the serving counter of the café and continued as he poured three glasses of water. "During the past twenty years, baby boomers have been busy spending beyond their means and piling up excessive amounts of personal debt."

As he came back to the table with the water, I thanked Mike for his hospitality and drank enough to clear my throat. "We can certainly relate to the overspending and not saving enough," I said.

Mike continued, "While personal net worth was rising due to increases in real estate and the stock market, everything looked fine. However, small cracks in the 'spend today and worry about it tomorrow' mentality have turned into gaping holes. With the promise of rising asset values gone, so too are the spending habits of ninety million North American consumers."

"What is the real significance of that, Mike?" I asked.

"Well, just think about the boom we have been in since the late 1980s. Think about all the industries that have flourished serving the baby boomers. Examples include real estate, home renovation, travel, cosmetic procedures, credit cards, and luxury retail. The baby boomers have been on a twenty-year spending spree, and entire markets have been created to meet their consumption appetite."

I could begin to see the connection between what Mike was saying and the way we spent our own money. Every year, life felt more expensive. I started to connect what Mike was saying to some of my own experiences. I heard a car outside and glanced nervously at the door. I hoped no one would come in before we finished our chat. Fortunately, it was just someone turning around.

"A few years back, I wanted a Harley," I said. "Mainly because a few of my friends had purchased one, and I thought it would be great fun to revisit my youth. I remember my local Harley Davidson dealer being totally swamped with orders, and their high-flying stock was the darling of many stock portfolios. I never did buy one, but from time to time I would visit the dealer and dream a little. The manager at the local dealership told me recently that they were not doing very well and were changing their corporate focus to global expansion."

"That's right, Don," Mike said. "Harley Davidson is a great example of how baby boomers created a comeback story for a company and its stock price. And it's also a great example of how a shift in demand, declining appetite for debt, and a reduction in discretionary consumption can derail a company and the stock price. Now imagine these types of spending shifts spreading across the North American consumption-based economy."

"I have heard about the use of *demographics* as a key forecasting tool for the economy. Is this what you are referring to, Mike?" inquired Mary.

"Yes," he replied. "One of the key ingredients to my personal success has been the study of how demographics impact economic cycles and economic trends. I don't believe that demographics can be used in isolation to attempt to define economic trends or financial bubbles. Along with some basic economic and personal financial principles, demographic science can be an extremely useful tool. Especially since the baby boomers are the largest demographic group in the North American economy."

"I get that," Mary replied enthusiastically. "Just like we traded up to our dream home and have watched our friends do the same thing. It seems uncanny that we are all talking about or making similar decisions."

"Yes," Mike agreed, "uncanny, but somewhat predictable when you understand demographics."

"So what you are saying is that we can use this information to be ahead of a trend and profit?" continued Mary.

"Well, remember it's not just demographics," Mike said. "You also have to take into account economic factors that I will explain later. You also need a strategy and a plan you can stick with in both good and bad financial times."

I was getting excited at this point. "So now we have the average baby boomers very close to age sixty. Doesn't that put us into a period when they will be saving more and spending less?" I asked.

"Yes," replied Mike. "Now here's a question for you to answer when we meet again in a couple weeks: 'What are the consequences of the largest consumer group in our history making the shift from overspending to oversaving?'"

Mary and I got up to pay our bill, but Mike told us this one was on the house. We set our next meeting and thanked Mike for his generosity.

Oversaving

Two weeks had gone by since our first meeting with Mike. On many levels, nothing in our life was different. The financial stresses were piling up, and my pending downsizing was still very much my main concern. However, Mary and I had somehow been reenergized to take control of our financial future. We poured ourselves into researching trends around the baby boomer lifestyle.

As we prepared for our meeting with Mike, we had a bunch of facts but were not really sure how to put it all together. On Wednesday, we put the information in a folder and headed out to Café Milano. We ordered our usual coffees.

"I can see from the notes you have brought with you that you have been doing some research," Mike said with a smile.

"Yes, both Don and I have been devouring anything we can get our hands on related to the baby boomers," beamed Mary.

"So, let me hear what you have," Mike replied.

I cleared my throat and fidgeted in my seat before beginning. "The bulk of the baby boomers were born between 1946 and 1950. Every ten seconds, starting in 2008, a new baby boomer will be joining the ranks of those eligible to claim social security. Understanding the distribution of this population is important when trying to estimate its effect on real estate, the stock market, and planning for retirement. Many demographic researchers attribute the economic boom that started in the early 1980s to the rise of the baby boomers' spending power and access to easy credit. This includes the rise in real estate and the stock market. Many of these same researchers are calling for the bursting of the financial bubble as the bulk of this group enters their peak savings years."

I stopped to clear my throat and looked up from my notes at Mary. She nodded for me to continue. "The surging economy and stock market may reverse and turn into a contracting economy and *bear market* for stocks as baby boomers change their spending and savings patterns. A general prevailing theory goes that as baby boomers retire, they will need to start reining in their spending. They will no longer be saving a measly 1 percent of their income. Instead, they will be spending more on health care and allocating more to their retirement assets. The demand for aggressive financial assets will slow as baby boomers cash out some of the trillions of accumulated retirement assets to fund living expenses. This would reverse the baby boomers' previous experience of an unusually large group of buyers that drove up demand and helped propel prices upward."

I took a sip of my coffee. "Mary, would you like to wrap it up?" I asked.

Mary, who was responsible for putting the bulk of our notes together, brought our analysis to a close. "It is well documented that many baby boomers have not saved enough for retirement, and many of those that did save and invest saw their assets decimated by the three-year bear market in stocks from 2000 to 2002."

Mary paused, lifted her head up, and looked at Mike. "This is basically our own situation, Mike," she said. Then she continued, "According to the experts, this will not only result in less spending, but also trigger a shift to more conservative investments, creating a downturn in financial assets and financial markets. In short, their predictions paint a picture of the financial boom of the last twenty years coming to an end sometime in the next decade."

"Bravo," Mike said. "So, how then do you prepare for a slowdown or a reversal of the biggest financial boom of our recent history?" He stood up and stretched his back. "My wife and I have recently taken up Bikram yoga. This is the hot yoga method made popular in California. It's a baby boomer thing, you know."

"What is?" I asked.

Mike smiled and continued with his stretch. "Fighting the aging process, living healthier and longer. This is part of the baby boomer conundrum. We are all planning to live longer and healthier lives and retire earlier. Using very simple math, we are all going to spend much longer in retirement, requiring more capital to fund our lifestyle."

I thought back to my father retiring at age sixty-four with a good pension plan and living until age seventy-two. He died of cancer, after a short but difficult battle. Back then, seventy-two seemed really old. Funny how your definition of "old" changes as you move into your fifties.

Mike smiled and continued, "Let's go back to your notes. You have painted the worst-case scenario very well indeed. But you have not given me the other side."

"What do you mean?" I queried.

"The North American baby boomer represents a group of about ninety million individuals. This number is a drop in the bucket in terms of the global population. In the new era of global financial markets and global consumers, the baby boomers may have less sway and less of an impact."

Mary nodded in agreement.

"Many books written about the baby boomers in the 1980s and 1990s missed the mark on some major financial trends. They made forecasts about financial markets and financial sectors that never panned out. That's why I cautioned you about solely relying on demographic analysis. You need a broader perspective, with demographics as one arrow in your quiver but certainly not the only one."

Mary asked, "Can you give me an example to make this clear for me?"

"Of course," replied Mike. "If we go back to your notes, you mentioned the significant impact the bear market in stocks from 2000 to 2002 had on your own savings. It's estimated that during this bear market, over one trillion dollars of net worth was lost in less than three years. Hundreds of thousands of individuals saw their life savings and their retirement funds wiped out in a short period of time. Did this loss of wealth have anything to do with demographics or the baby boomers not wanting to own stocks?"

"Based on what we just discussed, I guess the answer is no," I said. "Which, to be honest, is really quite confusing."

"It's confusing if you think solely in terms of demographics," replied Mike. "The technology sector in late 1999 and early 2000 had become extremely overvalued. The stock prices and stock valuations were clearly unsustainable for the long term, no matter how much demand there was from baby boomers and other investors. If you did not have a decent understanding of economic cycles and stock market valuations, you probably made some very big mistakes and lost a good chunk of your wealth."

I watched Mary's face as she considered this. "I think I get it, Mike," interjected Mary. "You can know that the baby boomers may be driving spending or certain business sectors, but you need to make sound financial choices as well."

Mike nodded in agreement, "Yes, Mary, you got it. Since the early 2000s, health care stocks, which were supposed to go up in a steady fashion according to many demographic experts, have not performed well for investors. This goes totally against a demographic view of the health care sector. In fact many books were written on the subject and many investment vehicles were created to capture the trend, but the opportunity never came to fruition."

"Okay," I replied, "I now follow your logic. But what are we supposed to do?"

Mike moved behind the front counter of his store. He brought over one of Café Milano's menus and plopped it on the table with some dramatic flair. "First, you need to understand that demographics is only one arrow in your quiver. Secondly, you need to understand the major financial risks facing the baby boomer generation. Finally, you need to have a strategy and a process to mitigate those risks while seizing opportunities."

"That sounds pretty complicated," I replied. I could tell by the slumping of her shoulders that Mary concurred.

"Well, it could be," Mike said, "but the good news for you is that I have been using this approach since my early days on Wall Street, and it has worked well for me ever since. Throughout the booms and busts of the last thirty years, I have made mistakes, but overall my approach has allowed me to better mitigate my risks and take advantage of opportunities despite financial market conditions."

"I think that's all we really want. Better protect what we have created, grow it in a safe and prudent manner, and make sure we can maintain our lifestyle in retirement," Mary said.

Mike leaned over and picked up the previously tossed menu. "This menu is forecasting some very bad things coming our way. I don't think you are even remotely prepared for what you will be facing. Next week I will give you my forecast of the future."

We shook hands with Mike and left feeling excited about the progress we were making but also concerned about some of the tough choices ahead of us.

4

The Mocachino Meltdown

A week had gone by since our last meeting with Mike. I spent the bulk of the week preparing for my corporate downsizing. The best-case scenario would be a severance package of one year's salary, and the worst case would be a much smaller balance with some unemployment benefits.

Mary had devoted a number of hours to study and research the topics discussed with Mike. Trying to focus on the positive, I realized that at least Mary and I were communicating openly and honestly about our finances. This was something I could hold onto while the loss of my career appeared totally out of my control.

As we walked into Café Milano for our next meeting with Mike, I smelled something totally different. It was a lighter and sweeter smell than I recognized. "Something smells different, Mike," I said.

"These are organic espresso beans," Mike replied from behind the counter. "Smell great, don't they?"

"Yes, they do," I replied.

Not only was the smell different, but I noticed a number of changes to the lines of coffee offered in the café and also a change in many of the banners and posters in the store. "Fair trade, organic, and local sourcing?" I inquired.

"Yes," Mike shot back as he joined us in front of the serving counter. "These are all baby boomer trends that I am capturing here at Café Milano. We have also gone organic with our entire food menu and our cleaning supplies."

"Wow, Mike, that's fantastic," Mary said.

"It's part of my focus on sustainable wealth and sustainable business," Mike said.

"It's impressive and comforting to know that entrepreneurs like you actually care about something other than making a profit," I said.

"Actually, Don," replied Mike, "contrary to popular opinion, the capitalist system is the gateway to the massive changes required to create a sustainable future. But let's leave that discussion for another day."

Mike passed over two cups of coffee and said with a smile, "Organic, nonfat, fair trade, vanilla mocacchino. How is that for over-the-top baby boomerism?"

I couldn't help but chuckle. It is a little strange that we have collectively made coffee such an obsession. I was reminded of the day that I took my dad, a veteran of World War II and a child of the Great Depression, out for coffee and dessert. After taking one look at the menu, he promptly walked out. There was no way any of his ilk would spend four dollars on a cup of coffee.

"The nonfat vanilla latte, one of the most expensive coffee items on our menu, has not been selling well. In fact, over the past six months, sales are down 50 percent. That's not surprising for me, but I can bet you some of the large chain coffee shops are experiencing the same trend, and they are probably deeply worried about it," said Mike.

"Why is that, Mike?" asked Mary.

"I call it my unofficial *leading indicator*," Mike said with a grin.

"Leading what and indicating what?" I asked, clearly displaying my lack of economic prowess.

"An economic leading indicator is something that predicts what may be coming down the pipeline," Mike said. "It is a signal of a change that may be coming for the better or the worse. Examples of leading indicators include production workweek, building permits, unemployment insurance claims, inventory changes, and stock prices. There are also coincident indicators, which change about the same time as the overall economy, and lagging indicators, which change after the overall economy. Leading indicators can be very useful if you can integrate them into your financial decision making."

"I see," Mary replied as she wrote her notes more quickly to keep up with Mike.

Mike continued, "As a street-level merchant, I am experiencing a large decline in my high-end and high-margin sales. When people choose to no longer purchase a four-dollar cup of coffee, it signals that the economy may not be doing so well, despite what our politicians would like us to believe. It tells me that changes are coming and I need to make adjustments."

"That makes a lot of sense to me," I said. "Given our current situation, I have noticed how Mary and I have been cutting back on what used to be normal everyday purchases. It wasn't that we designed a big cutback plan but more a daily gradual approach to focus our spending on necessity and not so much on luxury."

"Exactly," Mike said. "Regular coffee sales are still stable, but our higher-end items are falling dramatically. If my livelihood depended on this store, I would be very worried."

"I imagine this change of spending habits is taking place across the entire economy?" questioned Mary aloud.

"Now you're thinking on your feet," Mike said with a big smile. "These types of changes in spending habits are important clues to potential changes in consumer behavior and the economy as a whole. Of course, my store does not represent the economy in its entirety, but it can be used as a clue for the discerning individual."

"Does this tie into your discussion of the boom and bust cycles of capitalism?" Mary asked.

"Correct," Mike replied. "I believe that big changes are on the way."

"Can you paint us an overall picture of what you think is coming?" I asked, leaning forward.

Mike paused before speaking. "There is a Zen saying that goes something like this: 'In every danger lies the seed of an equivalent opportunity.'"

Motioning us to join him at the nearest table, Mike continued, "The risk of a major global economic downturn is rising. The downturn may be particularly difficult, as the current boom has lasted so long and has been so large. Most individuals are painfully unprepared and will suffer greatly. There is great opportunity for those who are prepared and great danger for those who are not."

The door opened, and a group of students carrying their laptops sauntered in. We quickly set our next meeting date and took our coffee to go.

5

A History of Bubbles and Troubles

Mary and I had been arguing less and collaborating more. Inspired by our dire financial situation, we were working together as true partners. As we approached Café Milano the following week, we chatted about the surreal nature of the chance encounter with Mike and the meetings that had followed. Mary's advice was to not overanalyze the situation and simply go with the flow.

I moved to open the front door to the café but found it locked.

"Hey there," bellowed a voice from the distance.

We both looked around and could not see anyone.

"Up here," the voice shouted.

We looked up to see Mike standing on the roof of Café Milano.

"Be right down," he called out.

After a few minutes, Mike opened the door and welcomed us in. The smell of freshly baked muffins filled the room. A combination of blueberry and chocolate was too hard to resist.

"I think we are going to have to try some of those," I said, pointing to the steaming tray of muffins on the far serving counter. "They smell heavenly."

Mike moved toward the muffin tray and carefully placed the dozen muffins on a serving tray for us to choose what we wanted.

"What were you doing up there on the roof?" Mary asked.

"Inspecting the roof for a new solar panel installation," Mike said.

"Solar panels on your roof?" I asked. "Is that a good investment?"

Mike nodded and replied, "Forget 'Greed is good.' I think one of the major investment themes for the next decade is 'Green is good.' The

Paul Ghezzi

coming decade is going to usher in a renewable energy infrastructure boom. Wind power, solar power, utility grid enhancements, biomass, and much more."

Before I could get any details out of Mike, he asked us to join him in the library section of the café. Not more than two hundred fifty square feet in size, the library section had three comfortable leather chairs and included four separate bookcases. As Mike explained to us, this was his collection of favorite books that he wanted to share with his patrons.

"I have to be honest," said Mike. "I am all for the technology of today, but there is absolutely no comparison to holding a fifty-year-old book in your hands versus a digital computer screen."

Moving her right hand gently across the many neatly organized books, Mary replied, "I fully agree."

"So, are you ready for a history lesson?" chirped Mike.

"History was never my favorite subject," I replied. I was still hoping for a quick fix to get past our financial problems and was not excited about a history lesson.

"I think you might enjoy this history lesson. It's filled with excitement, danger, intrigue, and turmoil," Mike said as he pointed to two full rows of books behind him. "The books that I am pointing to provide a vast amount of information about our financial history, dating back to the creation of the very first stock exchange in Antwerp, Belgium, in 1531. As George Santayana, the Spanish-American philosopher, once said, 'Those who cannot remember the past are condemned to repeat it.'"

"That's amazing," I said. "Stock exchanges have been around that long?"

Mike nodded and replied, "One of the problems with our society is that we are so hooked on instant information and instant gratification that we have lost touch with our past."

"I am information overloaded," Mary replied. "It's the combination of all the information and the fact that much of it is contradictory. Invest, don't invest. Buy, sell. Stocks, bonds. Up, down. I think we have just given up and have tuned it all out."

"You are not alone, Mary," Mike replied. "Most people are so overwhelmed that they are tuning out as well, and just hoping for a positive outcome to their retirement problems. It's part of the retirement anxiety trap we have talked about."

"Is this where you think your history lesson can help?" I asked.

"Yes," replied Mike. "The history of capitalism is boom to bust and bust to boom. While the nature of the crisis for each generation is different, the impact of the crisis is often similar. There have been numerous booms and busts over the past four hundred years, and I will share a few of the grander ones so that you can view our current environment with a greater sense of perspective."

While I enjoyed Mike's company and deeply appreciated our time together, I wanted more answers than lessons. Mary appeared to be less perturbed than I was about the pace at which we were moving.

"Mike, do you think this is necessary?" I said. "Being totally pragmatic, isn't it different this time around?"

Mike paused before responding and leaned back in his chair. "Well Don, why don't you answer that question after we take a brief jaunt through a history of bubbles and troubles? An *investment bubble* is an investment phenomenon associated with a parabolic upward move in underlying asset values. An investment bubble occurs when investors put so much demand on an underlying asset that they drive up the price beyond any rational reflection of its actual worth."

Mary nodded in agreement and asked, "Can you share some specific examples?"

Mike replied, "Have you heard of the tulip mania? In the middle of the sixteenth century, the first tulip bulb was introduced into Europe from Turkey. The tulip was confined to the gardens of the nobility of the day, making them quite scarce to the general public. As tulips made their way to the general public, supply remained scarce and variations of the tulip increased. This was a classic example of growing demand with limited supply, which is a precursor to every financial bubble. The frenzy surrounding the speculation in tulips reached the point where ordinary individuals were willing to risk two or three years worth of their income on the hope that tulips would continue to increase in value. When supply eventually dwarfed demand, the buyers disappeared and speculators were left with devastating losses. Investors demanded government action, and once-admired speculative traders were treated as the dregs of society."

"It sounds like the tulip craze was similar to the Great Depression and the stock market crash of 1929," said Mary.

"Quite perceptive, Mary," Mike replied. "The Golden Age, the period from 1920 to 1929 that preceded the Great Depression, was characterized by mass production, automation, personal consumption, and great gains in productivity. It was the onset of a new age of prosperity ushered in by western industrial capitalism. Like the booms and busts that preceded it and followed, this period is widely recognized for stock and real estate valuations reaching extreme highs and moving dramatically above historic averages. During this time individuals were willing to risk as much as they could borrow to participate in the stock market boom. When the selling started and the buyers retreated, there was nothing that could save the stock market. The meteoric rise in stock values and instant wealth evaporated more quickly than anyone could have imagined. From peak to trough, the stock market lost 90 percent of its value. It took a total of twenty-six years before the market recovered to the highs set right before the crash."

While Mary appeared to be enjoying the conversation with Mike, I was feeling tired and somewhat claustrophobic. I needed to get some air.

A chime sounded in the kitchen and Mike stood up. "That's my queue to run," said Mike. "I have some cookies waiting to be removed from the oven. Why don't you two do some more research on investment bubbles, and we can discuss it in our next meeting. I am away next week taking care of some personal business, so let's set the meeting for two weeks from today."

We purchased some muffins for home and thanked Mike for his time.

As we walked to our car, Mary asked, "What's wrong?"

"I guess I wanted more insights into our current situation as opposed to a history lesson," I replied.

"Don't worry, Don," Mary said. "I trust Mike. Remember what he said about understanding the past so we don't repeat the same mistakes."

I nodded and grabbed hold of Mary's hand. "Keep reminding me to stay focused on what we really want. You are better at it than I am."

More Burst Bubbles

It was the first time we received an e-mail from Mike. Instead of meeting him at Café Milano for our next scheduled time together, he requested that we meet with him at the corner of Fairfields Drive and Summerhill Street. I could not remember anything in that area that would be appropriate for our meeting.

During the week prior to our next meeting with Mike, I received my severance package. It was less than I expected, but it was better than my worst-case scenario. It was hard to swallow that all my loyalty amounted to was six months of salary and medical benefits. Mary was doing the best she could to pick up extra hours at the community bank, but most of the other employees were looking for the same. Every little bit helped as we worked together to cut our expenses.

We started our drive to meet with Mike, and I said, "Thanks for doing the bulk of the research for the meeting. I'm sorry that I wasn't more help, but I just have not been able to focus this week."

Mary replied, "I understand. It's the finality of your job and restructuring. But I want you to start giving time to thinking about solutions as well. We need to make some big changes."

"You're right," I grumbled.

When we arrived at the corner of Fairfields and Summerhill, all I could see was a vacant piece of land to the north of us and a vacant strip mall to the right. A gas station was located to our left and a sprinkling of older homes to the south. This was the part of town that was the last to be redeveloped and was generally considered a lower-income neighborhood.

"Do you think he meant here?" I asked. "Maybe he made a mistake."

In the distance I could hear the rumbling of what sounded like a truck and the faint smell of burned French fries in the air. I looked toward the sound and noticed a green truck driving toward us. As the truck approached, the smell of French fries grew stronger and developed into a smell that might be more common in a greasy spoon diner.

"Hi guys, good to see you," Mike said. He climbed out of his SUV and headed toward us.

"What is that smell, Mike?" I asked. "Is it coming from your truck? Is something wrong with your truck?"

Mike burst into laughter. "That's my French fry machine!"

"Your what?" Mary queried with her hands on her hips.

Mike stopped laughing. As he sauntered over to us, he pointed toward the truck. "It runs on a biodiesel fuel blend made from vegetable oil that was used to cook French fries. I have a deal with Josh Winters, who owns the Two-Quarter Restaurant in town, to sell me his old vegetable oil so I can run my truck with it. I fitted the truck with a conversion mechanism over a year ago and have not been to a gas station for fuel ever since."

"Amazing," I replied. "The smell is hard to get used to, but I assume you are getting some other benefits?"

Mike replied, "Our love affair with fast food may be part of the solution to ending our oil- and carbon-based addiction. Biodiesel may be the definitive green fuel of the future. It's derived from low-value agricultural products, degrades rapidly, and is low in harmful emissions."

"This goes back to your point about the capital system being part of the solution and not the problem?" Mary asked as she inspected Mike's truck.

"Exactly," Mike replied. "We know as a society we have to get more sustainable with our energy sources and better manage how we produce and use energy. I believe we are on the verge of moving beyond our oil addiction. We can do it."

Mike paused and circled around us. "Take a look over to your right. What do you see?"

"An empty strip mall," replied Mary.

"That's right," replied Mike. "This multimillion-dollar development has gone bust and is a shining example of the investment bubble in commercial real estate. Too many retail shopping centers and too much supply of leased premises."

Mary replied, "Sounds like what we have discovered in our research."

Mike said, "I am interested to hear what you have put together."

Mary pulled out her note sheets from her pants pocket and began to read aloud. "There have been numerous investment bubbles following the Great Depression. They include the Japanese real estate bubble, the U.S. savings and loan bubble, the Internet bubble, and the most recent real estate bubble. The old saying 'What goes up must come down' does not quite capture the voracity of the bursting of a financial bubble. While it is true that the deflation of asset bubbles results in asset declines, the declines are better characterized by a violent bursting of the original bubble. This creates a situation where the majority of investors are trying to exit the investment bubble at the same time, and consequently sellers of assets flood the market. Attempting to avoid increasing losses, investors hope to unload their declining assets to other investors, but buyers are nowhere to be found."

Mike commented, "That's a good characterization. Having experienced all of those investment bubbles firsthand, I know it is not a pleasant experience when the bubble bursts."

Mary nodded and continued reading from her notes, "If we look at these examples of financial bubbles forming and bursting, we find similar patterns: the promise of instant riches, the forecast of increasing asset values in perpetuity, the promise that the new bubble is different from those of the past, the rise in debt levels as part of the speculative frenzy to participate in the bubble, the eventual bursting of the bubble, scandals arising from both private and public sectors, and the loss of massive amounts of wealth in a short period of time."

Mike smiled and said, "So, give me a defining statement that sums up a financial or investment bubble."

Paul Ghezzi

"Let me give this a go since Mary has done the heavy lifting," I said. "It's pretty clear that financial bubbles are part of our economic past and will be part of our economic future. What makes them hard to identify as they become overinflated and are preparing to burst, is that they become accepted as part of our social landscape. One person who believes a particular asset class or investment is undervalued will not cause a bubble. However, the group mentality—the crowd mentality—helps give birth to and sustain a speculative bubble; no one wants to believe that it can burst."

Mike began clapping and flashed his signature smile. "Bravo and well done, Mary and Don. You got it."

I wanted to pin Mike down with some specific questions that related directly to our finances as opposed to a general discussion. I started to speak, "Mike, I really want to know ..."

Just then Mike's phone buzzed, and he apologized in advance of taking the incoming call. "It's my wife, and I have to run. Great work, and I will e-mail the next time for us to meet."

Mike and the French fry smell were gone, and I was left with some burning questions.

- 6 -

The Lottery Syndrome

Mike had sent us an e-mail a few days ago to meet him at Café Milano. He asked us to pick up three lottery tickets and bring them with us. While we found this very strange, we did as he asked.

As we entered the café, we found Mike stretched out in one of his yoga poses.

"Good morning," Mike said, untangling himself from what appeared to be a very complex yoga position. "You can never do too much yoga." He stood up, stretched his fingers toward the ceiling with his straight back, and exhaled deeply. "Did you remember to bring the lottery tickets?"

Something triggered a sense of fear and anger in me. It could have been watching Mike practicing yoga in a relaxed and carefree manner, or it could have been the reference to the lottery tickets.

"Mike, I have to tell you that I am totally frustrated," I said as wiped my forehead with my hand. "We have come to you to ask for some help, and you have been very gracious with your time, so please don't take this the wrong way. While my academic understanding of how dire the financial landscape is for most baby boomers has improved, I don't feel like you are actually helping us. I am more nervous now than when we first met. I don't know what to do and just want a simple solution to our financial situation."

As soon as I finished my sentence, I regretted letting my frustration and fear get the best of me. It was my anger and frustration percolating to the surface and me forgetting to turn on my brain filter.

Mary sat in silence. While she did not say a word, her body language conveyed everything. I knew exactly what she was thinking, and she was not happy.

Mike smiled and in a relaxed manner replied, "Don, I appreciate your candor, but the truth is that you are looking for an easy way out of a life that you have created. Anyone with an ounce of integrity will tell you outright that a quick fix is not possible. Studies show that within five years of winning the lottery, 85 percent of all lottery winners will be right back to the same financial position they were in prior to winning. If I gave you an investment opportunity that made you instantly rich, it wouldn't change anything over the long term. To get what you want, you will need to make fundamental changes to your consumption, saving, and money management behaviors."

I swallowed my pride and my frustration. "I guess that's the lesson of the lottery tickets," I said as I held them in my hands. "I apologize for my outburst, and you are totally correct. It's easier to blame someone else or look for an easy way out of our problems, instead of owning up to the changes that we need to make. It's that get-rich-quick mentality looking for an easy way out with no work on our part."

Mike moved behind the sink and filled three glasses of water that he brought over to the table. "It may sound trite, but the truth is that most baby boomers have been overspending and overleveraging themselves in pursuit of instant gratification and instant wealth."

I squirmed in my seat. This was a sensitive issue for me. There was no doubt that we had been living as if the good times would never end.

Mike continued, "Statistically you have a much better chance of getting struck by lightning than you do of winning the lottery. This means that personal responsibility and accountability are the most important attributes you must develop in relation to your desire for financial independence."

"It's hard for me to admit our failures," I said with a mixture of anger, resentment, and grief gripping my heart. "I feel like I have failed." I could not contain my emotions, and tears began to roll down my face.

As I looked down, Mary grasped my hand firmly. She began to cry and said, "We are in this together. We have made mistakes together, and we are going to get through this together."

I needed that reassurance more than she will ever know. I collected myself and wiped the tears from my eyes, feeling both relieved and embarrassed.

"I understand your frustration," replied Mike sympathetically. "I believe part of the challenge for all of us is how we choose to define success and failure."

"What do you mean?" I asked.

Mike said, "There are two billion people outside of North America who live on less than one dollar per day. I would say by that standard that you have done quite well."

"While that's a staggering contradiction to the way we live in North America, I don't understand how that applies to the mess that we are in," I responded.

Mike replied, "Success and failure are relative terms. You have created a lifestyle that is not sustainable, and in the process labeled what you have been able to create, up to this point, a failure. If you continue on this path, you will experience the same results."

"How do we change this?" asked Mary.

"You have to take control of your life and your finances," replied Mike. "You need to understand that no one is coming to your rescue. You need to understand the new rules of the game of wealth. But most importantly, you need to let go of the past and move forward in a spirit of optimism and possibility."

"Easier said than done," I replied, unable to fully embrace most of what Mike was sharing.

"Nothing I have ever accomplished in my life that was truly worth something has been easy," Mike said. "The path of personal responsibility and accountability is filled with many obstacles. But what is the alternative?"

"Hope for a rebound in the stock market and real estate market, and maybe a good dose of government intervention," I replied. "Surely things have to get better from here."

"I wish I could agree with you, Don," replied Mike. "What is heading toward us is the perfect financial storm, and its size and scope are beyond what most baby boomers are prepared to handle."

Mike looked at us and smiled. "I appreciate your sharing today. It means a lot to me that you trust me enough to do so. I have to run some errands now, but I will leave the choice up to you. Keep the lottery tickets and hope for a miracle, or be prepared for what is heading our way."

Mary and I left the café holding hands and talking about the concepts Mike had shared.

7

The Perfect Financial Storm

A week after our last meeting with Mike, the embarrassment of my outburst was still raw, both from a personal perspective and dealing with Mary's disappointment. I remembered what Mike had said about the seeds of chaos and opportunity and used my frustration as a catalyst for change. The point that Mike made about me wanting to take the easy road out really hit home. I was spending most of my time complaining about my job, globalization, the economy, the government, and anything else I could add to the list. The reality was that I could be using this same amount of energy looking for long-term solutions.

Following a gut feeling, I decided to take a trip to the local bookstore. I spent an entire afternoon researching the corporate trend, over the past twenty years, to downsize and outsource. What I experienced in my work was exactly the same experience that millions of employees had experienced as part of the new global economy.

"Mary, I have an idea," I shouted as I burst through the front door after spending the day researching.

Mary turned away from her computer screen. She was reviewing our financial balance sheet and personal cash flow statement for our next meeting with Mike.

"I think I have a real solution to my work problem," I said. "Not sure if it's going to fly, but it's better than playing the role of the victim."

"Don, what are you talking about?" asked Mary as she raised her eyebrows.

"No one knows more about the Agilent product line than me. I know every single detail about the manufacturing line and the product supply chain. I was responsible for some major improvements in the past five years," I said as I tried to contain my enthusiasm.

"I know that, Don," Mary replied. "Your reward was to be downsized, and the plant moved offshore."

"Yes. The reason they are making the move is to cut expenses, increase profits, and protect their products from global competition. This is the trend, and I can fight and complain or find a way out," I said.

"How so?" Mary asked, now standing up and listening attentively.

"I am thinking about pitching the company about taking me on for a one-year contract to manage part of the transition to the offshore facility," I said. "The one-year contract will provide a buffer for us to rearrange our financial affairs and our lifestyle to better meet our retirement plans."

"Well," Mary sighed. "I have no idea if they will accept, but it's better than doing nothing. What can it hurt to make the pitch?"

"Agreed," I said. "I will spend some time researching the advantage to me and the company and go in prepared."

"You know I cannot attend the next meeting with Mike as I have to meet our banker," said Mary. "It's the third time we have rescheduled, and I need to be there."

"No problem," I replied. "Hopefully I will have some great news to share with Mike as my idea comes to fruition."

Storm Clouds on the Horizon

Another week had gone by. While Mary was meeting with our banker, I was walking into Café Milano.

"Hi, Mike," I said as I walked briskly, almost skipping toward the front counter.

"Hey, what's with the off-the-charts energy this morning?" Mike asked, strolling out of the back room.

"I have some great news to share," I said. "But before I do, I want to apologize again for my outburst at our last meeting."

Mike waved his hand in the air and replied, "No more apologies. It's okay, and let's move on."

"Got it," I said.

"Well, before you share the news, where's Mary today?" Mike asked.

"Mary is meeting with our banker to prepare consolidated reports for our balance sheet and cash flows," I replied. "She is much better at that stuff than I am."

"Good to hear. It's important to have a clear picture of where you are today," Mike replied. "You have to know where you stand to chart your course for where you want to go. Now, give me the good news."

"Well, after my less-than-stellar performance at our last meeting, I took something you said to heart and put it into action."

"Do tell," replied Mike, leaning forward on the main counter.

"I pitched my company on hiring me as an independent contractor for the next year to help them with their offshore transition. I know I have a lot of intellectual capital that could really help them. They get to offload my medical benefits and severance, and I get to create a one-year buffer to put our financial affairs in order."

"Bravo, Don," Mike said. "You found the opportunity in the chaos. Did they take you up on your offer?"

"Not exactly what I had in mind," I replied. "However, they are interested in a nine-month contract with the option to renew for an additional six months. I also get a bump in pay as I am giving up my benefits; and with the assistance of my accountant, I get some fairly sizable tax benefits by becoming an independent contractor."

"Outstanding," Mike said. "How does Mary feel about this?"

"Well, she is not crazy about the extra travel," I replied. "But overall the idea of the time buffer is very positive. We are both feeling more relaxed and focused."

"Well, you have probably figured out that outsourcing our manufacturing base is a megatrend that is not changing anytime soon," Mike said. "Understanding trends like this is integral to better protecting and growing your wealth. Let me share five other megatrends that are converging to create the 'perfect financial storm' for the baby boomers."

"That would be great," I replied.

Mike picked up three sheets of paper and a CD resting on top of the main serving counter and passed them to me.

"I apologize, but I knew I would have to cut the meeting short this morning and prepared this CD for you and Mary," said Mike. "Please review the material, and we can discuss it in more detail when we next meet. I will send you an e-mail to confirm."

I left Café Milano and rushed home to share Mike's notes with Mary. I arrived home before she did but waited for her before studying Mike's information.

Mary came through the front door looking tired. "How did it go?" I asked. "You look exhausted."

Mary smiled, walked into the living room, and plopped herself on the couch. "It takes a lot of effort to be organized. I am tired but also feeling good," she replied.

"Mike had to cut the meeting short, but he gave me this CD that he recorded for us," I replied. "I wanted to listen to it together. Should I pop it into the CD player?"

"Of course," Mary replied. "Can't wait to hear what's next."

I put the CD into our stereo and turned up the sound as I reclined in my favorite chair. After a few seconds, we heard Mike's voice:

> *Don and Mary, my apologies for cutting the meeting so short this morning, but I am working on a project that needed my immediate attention. I prepared a summary of what I wanted to share with you and recorded it on this CD.*
> A few-second pause.
> *Heading our way is the perfect financial storm. Like a number of smaller waves converging to produce a megawave, there are five potential financial crises that are converging to produce this perfect financial storm in the coming decade.*
> A few-second pause.
> *I will start with the debt crisis. Economic growth in the United States over the past ten years has been averaging about 3 percent per annum. However, hidden in this growth rate is the greatest expansion of personal borrowing in our*

history. What appears to have been a robust growth rate was in part an illusion created by excessive borrowing. Most individuals have been buying whatever they wanted before they had the money to do so. Everyone else seemed to be doing it. This has resulted in many people taking on too much debt. This means, in financial terms, that they have prespent their future earnings. When the future comes, they will have to make the choice of living on less money or adding more debt, which makes the problem worse. To avoid the harsh truth, bankers did just what the government and the public wanted them to do: keep the game going.

Financial innovation on Wall Street, with easy credit markets and low interest rates, has given birth to a complex credit and debt derivatives market that may be valued at over five-hundred trillion dollars. The credit expansion, which has been part of the last twenty years of prosperity, is now pushing the global economy to its breaking point. In the past, a bank would keep one dollar of real capital on its books to support about twelve dollars worth of lending. Today that number, due to fancy and complex financial structures, is closer to thirty dollars. Debt makes financial returns look better on the upside and makes financial losses much more dramatic on the downside.

The implications will be a massive deleveraging and deflationary pressure. In the housing market, for example, when individuals can no longer pay their mortgage and the banks begin to foreclose, this leads to both asset and debt liquidation. With the ratio of household debt to disposable income at record levels, small changes in home values and the tightening of credit markets can have a big impact on the ability and willingness of individuals to pay back their debts. More foreclosures put downward pressure on home values, which in turn leads to increased foreclosures. This deleveraging spiral can have disastrous consequences for the overall economy, which has come to rely on excessive spending by individuals and leveraging for personal consumption.

A few-second pause.

Next I will discuss the real estate crisis. Household savings rates have been negative for more than a decade, with individuals spending their future earnings at a pace never seen before in our history. Hitting a peak in the early 1980s, personal savings rates have been in steady decline since then. Individuals have been borrowing against their homes, like personal piggy banks, to fund their consumption-driven lifestyle.

Using your home as a piggy bank is an invention of the new world of complex financial borrowing. Individuals have taken on too much debt and have used their homes as their financial backstop, on the assumption that their homes will continue to rise in value. When housing values go down, as part of normal cycles of economic expansion and contraction, the unwinding of the debt crisis will parlay into a more substantial real estate correction.

Too much easy access to debt has resulted in rising real estate values that are not sustainable over time. The price-to-income ratio is a key affordability measure for housing. It is most often calculated as the median house price to median familial disposable income, expressed as a percentage. This measure has historically hovered around a value of 3 or less, but in recent years has risen dramatically. In many geographic markets, the ratio has risen in excess of 10. A correction back to long-term averages would be devastating to many baby boomers and the economy in general.

While there have been numerous boom-to-bust cycles in housing, the current real estate crisis will have much more significant and sweeping ramifications across the economy. The difference this time is that baby boomers have experienced a historic rise in the value of their homes and the amount of personal debt that they are holding. Given the size and magnitude of the rise, the correction will be very severe. Most individuals who are betting on rising home values to fund their lifestyle or their retirement are woefully unprepared for potential housing value corrections on the horizon.

A few-second pause.

The third potential crisis I broadly define as the stock market crisis. Over the past twenty years, the stock market has become increasingly complex and less transparent. The emergence of hedge funds and financial derivatives has created more volatility. More individuals have their retirement assets and savings in the stock market, and many are banking on unrealistic returns to buffer their lifestyle.

The low-interest-rate environment has fueled an increasing appetite for risk, not only in real estate, but also in stocks. As with real estate, most individuals are under the misconception that stock markets always go up in the long term. They remain blissfully unaware that, over the past one hundred years, there have been many periods of substantial decline or of very little growth.

Historically stock markets have traded at around fifteen times earnings (referred to as the price-to-earnings ratio). This means that for every dollar of earnings generated by a company, an investor would be willing to pay fifteen dollars. In periods of economic distress, the price-to-earnings ratio has declined to single digits. In periods of economic boom, the price-to-earnings ratio has expanded to more than twenty. Today stock markets are trading above twenty times earnings. This means that investors are willing to pay twenty dollars for every dollar of earnings generated by a company. If we simply returned to the long-term average, we could easily experience a 30-percent decline in general stock values. If we were to enter a new period of economic distress, then we could experience a much more significant decline.

The theory that baby boomers will continue to chase stocks up and pay higher and higher price-to-earnings multiples does not hold up to reality. As evidenced by the crash in the technology sector from 2000 to 2002, baby boomers will sell their shares if they believe the trend is down.

Imagine retiring at a time when the stock market underperformed for five, ten, or twenty years. What impact would this have on your ability to maintain your lifestyle in retirement?

When you are withdrawing funds out of your portfolio in retirement, investment losses are magnified and can lead to a more rapid depletion of your capital. In retirement the ability to handle major shocks and recover is much less than when someone is in their early forties. The margin for error is also much lower.

The idea that it's always a good time to invest in the stock market is simply not the case. What you buy and when you buy it are very important to your overall success.

A few-second pause.

The fourth crisis is the pension and social security crisis. In just a very short period of time, the burden of protecting your wealth and growing enough wealth to fund retirement obligations has shifted almost completely to the individual.

From 1940 to 1970, the government was the main source looked upon to fund retirement plans. The workforce was not mobile, and the emphasis was on employment for life, with the government as a backstop for a modest retirement. From the early 1970s to the early 1990s, corporations took over with good defined-benefit pension plans. The notion was to get a good job and have a good pension for retirement. The benefits to be paid at retirement were defined in advance, providing comfort and security.

Starting in the early 1990s, corporations began to move away from issuing defined-benefit plans and began the mass migration to defined-contribution plans. Defined contribution plans, by their nature, offer very little security compared to a defined-benefit plan and are much cheaper to fund and manage.

During the decline in the stock market from 2000 to 2002, the pension crisis was revealed for a brief period of time. The problem quietly went away when stock markets across the globe trended back up from 2003 to 2007. Many experts believe that unfunded pension obligations are in the hundreds of billions of dollars. The expectation is that these obligations will be funded from future returns generated in the financial markets. A few years of subpar performance will expose these obligations once again. What exacerbates the problem is that these obligations will impact the bottom line of corporations and act as a drag on profits. Lower profits leads to lower share prices. It's a vicious cycle that gets worse with poor performance in the financial markets.

A defined-benefit plan carries great reward to the individual employee and great risk to the employer. A defined-benefit plan is a written contract by which an employer only or an employer and workers are required to make monetary contributions in view of providing the workers with retirement income. The amount of your pension income is set in advance according to a precise formula. The amount of the contributions is determined by the actuary who carries out the plan's actuarial valuation.

A defined-contribution plan shifts the risk to the individual employee and makes no guarantees for future sustainability and pension income. There is no way to know how much the plan will ultimately produce in terms of pension benefits or pension income. The funding costs are much lower than defined-benefit plans. That's a primary reason for the rise in popularity and use of the defined-contribution plan.

On the public funding side, the situation is even more worrisome. In 1950, there were seven workers per retiree; today there are five. From a simple math point of view, this means that there are increasingly fewer workers funding a massive amount of retirees. Perhaps gains in worker productivity and immigration can help offset some of the reduction in workers per retiree, but the size of the baby boomer population will make this an escalating crisis. It's estimated that the combined North American social security obligations over the next thirty years total between fifty to sixty trillion dollars.

A few-second pause.

The final crisis is the health care crisis. It is estimated that 20 percent of the population will be sixty-five years of age or older during the next twenty years. This is compounded by the problem that people are living longer than they used to and demanding more health care resources for a longer period of time. If you understand how the Pareto principle works, you will get a picture of what is to come. The Pareto principle was first associated with an observation made in the seventeenth century by an Italian economist who noted that 80 percent of the land was owned by 20 percent of the population. We now use this in our language as the 80/20 rule.

In relation to the health care system, it is believed that approximately 20 percent of the users of the health care system use up to 80 percent of the resources. This group of 20 percent *is widely skewed to the senior population. As people age, they need more health care services. Individuals in their early seventies use hospitals five times more as compared to their lifetime average. Those in the age group of seventy-five to eighty-five use hospitals twelve times more as compared to their lifetime average.*

The amount of strain placed on the government and on individuals to fund the health care system will be something that we have never experienced. Health care inflation is already running at three times the level of core inflation.

Who is going to fund this massive liability and how will the funding impact the economy and personal finances?

A few-second pause.

The perfect financial storm is something that baby boomers need to plan and prepare for. We can talk about this in more detail in our next meeting.

See you soon.

I walked over to the stereo and hit the stop button. I turned to Mary and said, "Wow, that was heavy. That was too much for me to absorb in one sitting. I will probably need to listen to that again."

"You and me both," replied Mary. "It all makes perfect sense, and yet we never gave any of this too much thought. Why is that?"

"Maybe because it's so big that most people can't grasp it or don't want to," I said.

"You are right," replied Mary, getting up from the couch. "Let's spend some time on these issues before our next meeting with Mike."

8

Financial Planning Myths Exposed

It had been two weeks since the last meeting with Mike. Mary had been working diligently to organize our financial affairs into a tidy binder. It was a difficult task to start, but the results were impressive. We were more organized and knew where we stood in relation to our cash flow, our savings, our equity, and our investments.

As we walked toward Café Milano, I was looking forward to a relaxed meeting with Mike to catch up on a number of fronts. I was also looking forward to a latte and muffin for breakfast.

Mike was waiting on the front steps of the café. "Good morning, and come on in. My apologies for the brevity of the last meeting," Mike said. "I had to take an emergency trip to Vietnam."

"Oh, you have business dealings there?" I asked.

"Oh no," replied Mike. "My wife and I operate a private foundation for impoverished children around the globe. We support numerous projects both locally and abroad dedicated to educating children in need. "There was a major problem with one of our community projects. Having been the connector between government officials and local tradesmen, I decided to go there and help resolve the situation."

"It's inspiring to see that you are doing such wonderful work, Mike," said Mary.

I nodded in silent admiration.

Mike blushed and replied, "Don't be so quick to share your praise, Mary. I was that brash, ego-driven guy who was focused solely on the size of his bank account. For a long period of time, the character of Gordon Gekko, played so well by Michael Douglas in the movie *Wall Street*, was a fair characterization of my life. I learned the hard way that there is no fulfillment in that world. There is never enough, and then it just becomes a game of more. It doesn't mean that I gave up all of my capitalist endeavors, but I do it for a bigger purpose than expanding my bank account."

We sat and absorbed what he was saying without uttering a word. Mike's sharing was causing me to take stock of my own life and how little I had been contributing to causes outside my own personal affairs. I was going to change this somehow.

"It's been awhile since we have shared a cup of coffee," said Mike. "Sit down and let me get you a fresh cup of our new free-trade brand from Africa. Bold and full-bodied, I might add."

"That sounds perfect, Mike," said Mary as she sat down at the table adjacent to the front door.

As Mike was making his way to the table carrying a tray with three coffees, he asked, "What did you think of my CD and the topic of the perfect financial storm?"

"I have to admit, for the first five minutes after listening to the CD, I was totally depressed," I said.

"That's the old Don," chuckled Mike. "The new Don can grasp the chaos, but gravitates to the opportunity. As Winston Churchill once said, 'A pessimist sees the difficulty in every opportunity; an optimist sees the opportunity in every difficulty.' I have given you an economic backdrop of the converging financial crisis associated with the baby boomers. This does not mean that you can't prepare yourself to take advantage of any potential opportunities."

"You're right," I replied as I sat back up. "It's the victim mentality that is hard to shake. The notion that one crisis can compound with another to create a much larger crisis is intriguing and frightening. But surely the world of financial planning offers a solution, doesn't it? I mean, our banker has kept us fully invested in spite of the bad times and the volatility. He keeps repeating the 'long-term' mantra."

"Well, how is that working for ya?" chided Mike as he delivered a poor Dr. Phil impersonation.

"Not very well," I concurred. "Mary has prepared an in-depth review of our personal balance sheet, cash flow, and investment portfolio. This has been both an eye-opening and painful experience."

"Clarity about a situation often requires you to come face-to-face with your fears," replied Mike. "The fact that you were able to work through the pain to gain the benefits of this exercise shows how far you have come."

Mary smiled and shot me a quick wink. While our finances had not improved much since our meetings with Mike, our strength and resolve had increased tenfold. We were now in this together, with a new level of honesty, communication, and commitment.

"Oh, sorry," said Mike. "I forgot to bring over the new pastries I wanted you to try. My wife has me watching my gluten intake. Let me grab a few of these pastries for you to try. Please continue," he said looking at Mary.

"Based on my review of our finances, our net worth has not grown in the past ten years," Mary said.

"Which, to be totally honest, is quite shocking," I chimed in.

"We seem to be on a roller-coaster ride in the stock market and real estate market," Mary said. "In addition, our banker has made changes at the wrong time, and other times no changes were made when they should have been. It's totally frustrating."

Mike returned to the table with some delectable-looking pastries. I had to try one and was most impressed. I motioned to Mary to have one as well.

"Who knew gluten-free could taste so good?" Mike asked.

"Agreed," I replied.

"The myth that stocks and real estate always go up in the long term is a failure of current financial planning wisdom," Mike said. "As history proves, bubbles can inflate dramatically in a short period of time and then burst just as quickly. Being on the wrong side of the bubble can result in substantial declines in your net worth."

"But what about the idea that interest rates are low and will remain low because baby boomers are demanding less financial debt and more financial assets?" I asked.

"Another myth," replied Mike. "Debt levels are soaring, and baby boomers are part of the trend. The prosperity ushered in by globalization has more to do with rising debt levels than a real increase in wealth for the average baby boomer."

"Can you elaborate?" I asked.

"In very simple terms, the 'globalization trade' has been to outsource labor to emerging economies, with low wage structures, in return for cheaper goods," replied Mike. "We have traded a good chunk of our manufacturing base and, in return, gained the ability to buy cheaper priced goods. You can get almost anything cheaper today than a few years ago."

"It strikes me that the long-term consequences of this trade-off are not very promising," I commented. "What is becoming increasingly clear to both Mary and me is that we have to become much better stewards of our own capital and we need to take control of our own financial destiny."

"This begs the question, Mike," Mary said. "Do you think globalization has been a bust all around?"

"It depends on which metrics you use to measure the success of globalization," replied Mike. "While capital markets have prospered and consumers have benefited from cheaper goods and lower inflation, the promise of trickle-down prosperity has not been fulfilled for most baby boomers. It comes down to global capital versus personal capital. I personally don't think most baby boomers have prospered as much as they thought they would. The rising tide of globalization has not lifted all ships equally."

It was sometimes hard to follow Mike in conversation. While I wanted to pause and reflect, he was often on to the next thought, so I learned to slow him down any chance I could. I had learned from previous meetings that I could get him to slow down or pause by asking him to elaborate on a specific topic. So I asked, "Can you elaborate?"

"The prosperity ushered in by globalization has not trickled down to the average baby boomer because they have misunderstood the rules of the game," Mike said. "They do not have enough savings and are not managing their capital in a manner to truly benefit. Statistics continue to show the affluent adding to their wealth in much higher percentage gains than the middle class. That's why you need to make some serious changes in your financial strategies. If you don't make those changes right now, you are risking your retirement."

"I can't help but feel we have been lied to or cheated in some way," Mary said, folding her arms over her chest. "We invested in the stock market for the long term, purchased our home on the assumption that real estate would continue to appreciate over the long term, worked very hard at our jobs, and saved enough to send our two children to university."

The front door opened, and I expected that this would be the end of our meeting. However, it was a delivery for Mike.

'Let me sign for this, and I will be right back," said Mike as he approached the delivery man and signed on a computer pad. Mike promptly returned to the table and continued where he left off.

"You are not alone, Mary," Mike said somberly. "You need to understand that you are using faulty information to make your financial decisions. In fact, most baby boomers will fall victim to the 'four great myths of financial planning.' These financial planning myths, which have been propagated during the course of the past twenty-five years, will not help you in the coming decade of financial crisis. The rules of the game have changed, and most baby boomers have not made the necessary adjustments."

"So in a nutshell, traditional financial planning is not going to work for baby boomers to help them get the results that they want?" Mary summarized.

Mike paused and said, "Do you remember Newton's third law of motion?"

"Something about action and reaction," I replied.

"For every action there is an equal and opposite reaction," replied Mike. "The massive bubble across all financial assets and personal debt, associated with the baby boomer lifestyle, is coming to an end. As the financial bubble was unprecedented in size, so too will be the bursting of this bubble and its many consequences."

"That intuitively makes sense," Mary said. "The bigger the size bubble, then the bigger the impact of the correction."

"Correct," replied Mike. "That's why I want you to watch this DVD. It was put together as a live teaching session by a friend of mine who is an economics professor and an old friend from my Wall Street days. I call him "the professor." His approach is a little dry and intense, but his message is very important."

"Okay," I replied. "I am looking forward to it."

Mary nodded in agreement.

"I will send you an e-mail for our next meeting date and time," Mike said.

"Thanks, Mike," Mary said as she reached out to touch his shoulder. "We probably don't say it enough, but we really appreciate the time you are spending with us. It has made a huge difference in our lives."

Mike replied, "The feeling is mutual."

We left the café looking forward to watching the DVD Mike had given us. I wondered to myself why he would feel any gratitude toward us. I often felt like we were imposing on his time.

An Economic Lesson to Remember

Mary and I arrived home and prepared a light lunch of tuna, cucumbers, and mixed green salad. We had been inspired by Mike to make better food and lifestyle choices. It wasn't anything he said directly, but more so in the manner in which he carried himself and took care of himself. We were even planning our first yoga class together.

"Are you ready for the DVD?" I asked.

"Yes," replied Mary. "I am curious about the four great financial planning myths."

I placed the disk Mike had given us into the DVD player and hit the play button. Mary was already seated on the couch with pen and paper in hand. I sat down beside her, mindful to give her enough room to take her notes. As the DVD began to play, we both took note of the classroom setting.

"Oh," said Mary. "It's a university classroom lecture. Wow, this takes me back to the good old days."

"Shhhhh," I said. "The professor is starting to talk."

The camera angle switched from a wide-screen shot of a university lecture auditorium to a close-up of the professor. He appeared to be in his late fifties or early sixties. He was slim and neatly kept. He was wearing a crisp blue polo shirt and gray trousers and looked comfortable and relaxed in front of the camera. It struck me that he was a man who had a fondness for order.

"Welcome to today's lecture on the four great financial planning myths. I am going to remind you to save your questions for the end of the lecture. Please keep the noise to a minimum. We are continuing our series on the impact of the baby boomers on the economy. This is the final lecture on this particular series, and the material we cover today will be part of your midterm exams."

The camera zoomed out to capture the professor and his PowerPoint presentation on a large white screen to his left.

"Let's begin with financial planning myth number 1, 'The stock markets always go up in the long term.'

"Please start the PowerPoint presentation," he said, speaking with someone off camera. He then took a small silver object from his right front pants pocket and pointed to the presentation screen.

"The average return of the stock market over the past one hundred years is approximately 8 percent per annum," he said. "However, there have been many periods of time lasting more than ten years where returns have been much lower than the average and periods of time where returns have been higher than the average. For the baby boomers, average returns are irrelevant. What is more important is what returns can they expect as they head into their retirement years based on the point in time that we find ourselves in."

"Next slide," he said with his attention focused on the screen. "A *bull market* refers to a prolonged period in which investment prices rise faster than their historical average. The term bull refers to a charging or zealousness with which markets advance. Bull markets are associated with prolonged periods of rising stock prices. Good economic news ignites frothy markets, and bad news is easily shaken off. In strong bull markets, investor optimism sometimes reaches a level of euphoria where paying up to thirty to forty times a company's annual earnings seems to make sense. Well above the long-term average as identified by the P/E ratio."

He paused to address his audience, "Please pay particular attention to the P/E ratio, as it will appear on your exam."

He moved his laser pointer toward the screen.

"The *price to earnings ratio (P/E ratio)* of a company's stock is a measure of the price an investor is willing to pay for profit earned by the company on a per share basis. A higher P/E ratio means that investors are paying more for each dollar of income. While not perfect in its use as a performance measurement tool, the P/E ratio is an important tool for investors with a long-term view. The average U.S. equity P/E ratio from 1900 to 2005 is approximately fourteen. What this means is that over the long term, investors have been willing to pay fourteen dollars for their share of one dollar of a company's profits."

The professor paused to take a sip of water from the water bottle located on the podium. He was now more animated in his presentation, switching between his laser pointer and hand gestures.

"A *bear market* is a prolonged period in which investment prices fall, accompanied by widespread pessimism," he continued. "The term bear refers to a clawing down of the market or a period of hibernation for growth. Bear markets are associated with large sell-offs in the financial markets and negative returns. Good economic news is greeted with only short-term glee, and bad economic news drives financial assets lower. The P/E ratio for stocks tends to be much lower in bear markets than it is in bull markets. This is because earnings growth is less robust and investor sentiment turns pessimistic."

The professor moved to the center of the stage and lifted both his right arm and left arm in the air. He then began to rock his arms up and down, doing his best to create the image of a scale moving in and out of balance.

He continued, "While the long-term average return of stocks over the past hundred years has been 8 percent, the truth is that over this period of time there have been numerous bull and bear markets. In this regard, the average return is irrelevant to the majority of investors, but even more so for baby boomers. Baby boomers do not have the time required for the long-term averages to prove themselves accurate. Please view the screen as I take you through a summary of the stock market's rise and fall over the last hundred years, using the *Dow Jones industrial average* as our proxy for the overall stock market."

The camera zoomed in on the presentation screen, and while we could hear the professor's voice, we could no longer see him.

"Let's look at the last hundred years as a graphical representation. From 1901 to 1921, there was no appreciation in stock values," he said. "From the period of 1921 to 1929, often referred to as the 'Roaring Twenties,' the stock market averaged spectacular gains in excess of 20 percent per annum. Investors were richly rewarded and stayed the course, remaining fully invested. The Roaring Twenties were followed by the Great Depression. From 1920 to 1932, the stock market lost 90 percent of its value and meandered until the end of World War II. Following the end of World War II, the stock market returned to a strong positive period. With the start of the baby boomer generation, the stock market averaged annual gains of approximately 14 percent per annum over a seventeen-year period. Buy-and-hold investors were once again richly rewarded."

The camera panned away from the screen to capture the professor in mid-drink.

"You can clearly see that bull and bear markets follow each other," he said. "The average returns often quoted by investment advisors and media miss this important consideration when evaluating returns and risk."

He used the laser pointer again, and the camera zoomed in for another presentation close up.

"I can personally attest to the fact that one of the toughest periods to be a long-term investor, in the stock market, was from 1966 to 1982," he said. "This is the period in our history marked by the Vietnam War and the first global oil shock. During this sixteen-year period, the stock market did not appreciate in value. Buy-and-hold investors did not benefit from their strategy. This terrible bear market was followed by the longest bull market of the past hundred years. The period from 1982 to 2000 brought an eighteen-year bull market. This period of time is an amazing part of our capitalist history. The introduction of both the personal computer and the Internet had a massive stimulus on productivity and corporate profits. Declining tax rates, declining interest rates, and a move to global trade and globalization provided massive fuel for the stock market. Those investors who employed a buy-and-hold approach were rewarded despite stock market corrections along the way."

As if prepared in advance, the camera zoomed in on the professor for a close-up. He paused as if he was adding dramatic effect.

"For the past ten years, starting in the year 2000, the stock market has been flat," he said emphatically. "We have had our share of mini booms and busts for the past ten years, but the value of the overall stock market ten years ago was the same as it is today. We now refer to this period as the 'lost decade.' I believe that for many reasons the stock market ten years from now may be at the same value as it is today or lower. As you can see, based on the summary of the past hundred years of stock market history, this scenario is quite possible."

He paused and put his hands on his hips. "Think about this and don't give me an answer today," he said. "What would the impact be on the baby boomers of a flat to negative stock market for the next ten years? Perhaps another 'lost decade'?"

I hit the pause button on the remote control and looked at Mary. "Wow, what do you think?" I asked, both concerned and keenly interested in Mary's response.

"Scary," replied Mary. "I have never seen anything like this before. We have always been told that investing for the long term is safe and secure. This changes all of my thinking about investing for the long term."

I nodded in agreement and hit the play button again.

The professor continued, "There is one major caveat to this part of the presentation. *Dividends* are significant from the perspective that, despite a falling or flat period in the stock markets, investors are being paid to wait. When factored in as part of the overall portfolio performance, returns are much improved. History can be a very useful guide for your future planning. We know that periods of strong stock market performance are followed by periods of poor stock market performance. The current financial planning mantra to stay invested in stocks for the long term, without any regard to these cycles, is both dangerous and flawed. The risks for baby boomers are even more significant as they will not have the time to recover from substantial losses in the stock market. If we do experience a substantial economic and stock market downturn in the coming decade, the majority of retirement plans will be in jeopardy."

This time Mary hit the pause button and stood up to stretch. "I need a coffee break after that. Do you want a cup as well?"

"Yes," I replied. "How do you feel about your mutual funds now?"

Mary moved to the kitchen and started to prepare two cups of our favorite instant coffee. "I don't feel good about them at all," she replied. "But you know that I have been uneasy about them for a long time. We just haven't done anything about it."

Mary returned with the coffee, and I hit the play button on the DVD remote.

"The next financial planning myth I would like to share is that 'home values always go up in the long term,' said the professor as he moved his laser pointer over the PowerPoint presentation. "Baby boomers, and the larger economy, have come to depend on the rising value of real estate and on increasing their debt load as a substitute for rising incomes. This is a trend that is not sustainable and, like the financial bubbles of the past, will eventually burst. The notion that home values trend upward in straight-line fashion is a dangerous myth. Real estate, as an asset class, has had many periods of rising value followed by declines in value. Real home prices, adjusted for inflation, were approximately 60 percent higher in 2004 than in 1890. But all of that increase occurred in two periods: the time right after World War II and the period since 1998. Other than those two periods, real home prices have been mostly flat or declining. Moreover, the overall increase is approximately in line with annual inflation."

The professor paused to take a drink from his water bottle and surveyed his audience before continuing. "The notion that real estate always produces much higher returns than inflation has been skewed by the real estate boom of the last fifteen years. Leaving the high interest rate era of the 1970s and 1980s behind, many have benefited from declining interest rates and massive expansion of debt and credit. During this time, many baby boomers came to rely on their homes as their primary investment and savings strategy. For many baby boomers, their home was their biggest investment. A decline in home values could be a trigger to a massive reduction in household net worth."

I hit the pause button on the remote and said, "I think we are both comfortable with this material. We have talked about this for quite some time now and agree with the professor. Can I fast forward?" With Mary's consent, I moved the presentation onward.

"To someone who appreciates a much more limited government role in our lives, myth number 3 is perhaps the most dangerous myth: 'The government will come to the rescue,'" said the professor. "The primary tools that governments have available to help manage economic cycles are: *monetary policy* (increase or decrease of the money supply) and *fiscal policy* (a change in the amount of taxes and governmental spending). Many nations choose monetary policy as their primary tool. It is less disruptive to market operations, and it is easier and quicker to implement since adjusting the money supply does not require legislative approval; changing the tax or spending structure requires legislative concurrence.

"Monetary policy is almost always carried out by a central bank. It is given the responsibility of juggling the sometimes conflicting goals of steady growth, low unemployment, and low inflation. Central banks can increase the money supply and stimulate the economy with lower interest rates. With credit readily available at low interest, consumers will tend to take out more loans for high-end goods, such as homes and cars, and businesses will invest more in facilities and employ more workers to meet the demand. This increase in money supply can result in higher-than-desired inflation. Central banks can also attempt to cool economic activity by announcing higher interest rates. A lower money supply can potentially rein in rising inflation. This is not an exact science, and even the best of intentions or policies can result in unintended consequences. Short-term interest rates are dependent on central bank and government policy; however, long-term interest rates reflect the ramifications of such policies on longer-term inflation.

"Governments can also use the tool of fiscal policy to help manage the economy. Fiscal policy includes both government spending and taxation. Large government deficits, when governments borrow to cover their excess spending over tax revenues, can be useful as a tool to manage economic bumps, but can also be inflationary. Government deficits have often been cited as useful in periods of recession; however, continued deficits result in growing national debt levels. The current U.S. national debt is approaching $14 trillion and is growing at $1.4 billion per day. The argument today against such extreme overspending by the U.S. government is that the inflationary pressure in the long term will be a major concern for future generations. Who is going to pay for these debts, and how will they pay for them?"

The professor paused and motioned to someone off camera to move to the next slide. He appeared somewhat agitated that the presentation was not on pace with his discussion.

"While governments appear to be much more responsive and have better information than ever, the nature of the boom-to-bust economic and business cycles has not changed," he said. "Business cycles move from expansion to contraction, and governments have never managed to be able to control these cycles. By preventing or delaying necessary adjustments in the economy, government intervention can lead to greater imbalances and greater boom-to-bust cycles. The *law of unintended consequences,* which states that any purposeful action will produce some unintended consequences, as it relates to the spiraling of government debt levels and a rise in debt-to-GDP ratios to historic levels is something that should be of great concern to you."

I pressed the pause button and excused myself for a much-needed bathroom break. Mary went into the kitchen and put some fresh fruit on a platter for us. I returned ready to hear about the final great financial planning myth.

Mary asked, "Remember what Mike said to us about excessive government regulation and government intervention in the economy and the impact on the government's finances?"

"Yes," I replied. "It's going to remain a huge political debate, but what's most important is that the requirement for personal responsibility has never been greater. There is no one coming to rescue us financially, and even if the government would like to play this role, there is no guarantee on the outcome."

I picked up a sliced apple from the tray that Mary had prepared and hit the play button.

"Last but not least in terms of financial planning myths is myth number 4: 'Deflation is a risk of the past,'" the professor said. "Deflation is generally defined as falling prices across a broad spectrum of assets. The end result of deflation is a general decline in nominal wealth across the economy. Contraction in asset values creates a negative wealth effect, where people tend to spend less because their assets are worth less. This leads to economic contraction and demand destruction. The most severe case of deflation we have experienced as a society was during the *Great Depression*. While very complex in nature and beyond the scope of today's presentation, the deflation associated with the Great Depression was primarily due to the stock market crash and a corresponding decrease in the supply of money. The stock market crash resulted in a flight to safety. Financial liquidity was taken out of the market place, and financial institutions failed, causing more fear and panic. The economy entered a deflationary cycle of economic contraction and job losses that led to more contraction. It can be argued that the governments of the time also made many policy blunders, with protectionist policies and not providing enough liquidity and stability to the financial marketplace."

The professor raised his right index finger as if to ask for everyone to pay close attention to what he was about to say. "However, the deflation boogeyman that we may be facing today comes from a different source. Traditional financial planning views the likelihood of a prolonged period of deflation as very remote, as the prevailing belief is that the government will come to the rescue. While the government can flood the financial system with money and protect banks from panicked investors, it is very difficult to stop a deflationary cycle over the long term. Especially given that the current risk of a deflationary cycle is related to too much debt in the global economy and the need to deleverage. Deleveraging refers to the reduction of debt levels across the economy. Deleveraging will be the trigger to massive asset declines across the investment spectrum, which will in turn create a negative wealth effect. When individual investors need to reduce their debt and repay their creditors, they have to sell something. When there are more sellers than buyers, asset values can decline in dramatic and rapid fashion."

The presentation screen adjacent to the professor went blank, and he motioned to the audience to remain quiet.

"That's it for today, but remember to hand in your assignments …" he said before I hit the stop button.

"How about a walk to clear our heads and talk about this stuff?" I asked.

"Great idea," Mary replied.

9

Preparing for the Best and Worst of Times

As we prepared for our next meeting with Mike, Mary and I had been making slow but steady progress to put our financial affairs in order. It wasn't that we were moving ahead in leaps and bounds, but we felt much more organized.

We received an e-mail from Mike to meet at the Oakhill Retirement Center. I thought it was a strange place for our meeting, but Mary's advice was to "go with the flow." Mary could not join us as she had taken on a few more hours at work, and I proceeded alone.

"Good morning," Mike said as he walked through the doors of the Oakhill Retirement Center. Glad you could make it. Come on in," he continued while holding the front door open for me.

"Morning, Mike," I replied as we shook hands and walked into the front lobby.

"You probably think it's a little strange that I wanted to meet here," Mike said.

"Yes, to be honest," I replied.

"Well, first of all, what do you think of the place?" inquired Mike.

The Oakhill Retirement Center was an example of the new breed of lifestyle retirement homes that had been popping up in recent years. Unlike government-run retirement homes, the new model was based on catering to a lifestyle of activity and seamless transition into a vibrant community. The décor was beautifully put together, and the pungent odor normally associated with retirement homes was replaced by a soothing combination of lavender and jasmine.

"I would say it's extremely well decorated, with a homey feeling," I replied.

"Yes, that's the look we were after," proclaimed Mike.

"You mean you own this?" I asked in a puzzled tone.

"No, not quite," grinned Mike. "I am a major investor in the project, but not the full owner or the operator."

"I see," I said, trying to take it all in.

Mike replied, "I have earned a very substantial return on my investment and also feel really good about making a difference in the community. I never invest my money without giving serious consideration to how my investment will impact the community. For me, it comes down to aligning my financial interests with my core values."

"The idea of investing in a retirement home never dawned on me, even though my friends talk about them in the context of their parents all the time," I replied.

"That's because you have been blinded by the four great financial planning myths," said Mike.

"That was an intense lecture, but very useful for us," I replied.

"I warned you about the professor, but he has always been intense," Mike said.

"Totally," I quickly answered. "But his presentation has caused us to take a second look at all of our investments and retirement funding strategies."

Mike nodded in agreement. "The idea that baby boomers can simply park all of their wealth in the stock market and plan their retirement around their house going up in value is flawed."

"Guilty as charged," I said. "You have really got us thinking about every facet of our finances, and we are in the process of making some big changes. The talk around deflation really spooked us."

Mike replied, "Deflation is like a pair of cement shoes on the economy. Think about home values declining in value along with the stock market. Think about consumer demand going down and the pressure on businesses to cut back to match the drop in demand. It's a downward spiral, where debt is no longer in vogue and cash is king. It will be the worst of times for those who are not prepared and the best of times for those who are in a position to take advantage of declining asset values across the board."

"Yes, I can see that," I said. "What about investing in this retirement home? Are there any opportunities here?"

"Let's get you moving toward a sound financial game plan before discussing specific investments," answered Mike.

"Okay," I replied, somewhat disappointed that my specific investment question had been pushed aside.

"Before we start, I have a few errands I need to run. Why don't you join me?" asked Mike.

Our first visit was to the main dining area, where one elderly gentleman sat on his own reading the newspaper.

"Hello, Jonah," Mike said. "This is my friend Don. Don, this is Jonah, resident poker shark and all-around ladies' man."

Jonah burst out in laughter. "Ha, ha … you might have me confused with someone else, Mikey boy. Are we on for that poker game tomorrow?"

"You bet," said Mike, tapping Jonah on the shoulder. "Gotta run, but see ya tomorrow."

Jonah barked, "Don't be a cheepo. Bring some of them good muffins from your place. Nice to meet you, Don."

"You as well, Jonah," I replied.

Following Mike around the retirement center was a profound experience. Instead of running errands, Mike spent over an hour visiting with various residents of the retirement community. The interactions were very much like the one with Jonah. The people we met all shined in the presence of Mike. It wasn't simply the fact that he had the gift to communicate with anyone he met, but it was the way he did it. It came from the heart, and it was real. It caused something in me to shift as I reflected on how stingy I was with my time and my community involvement.

"That was an amazing experience, Mike," I said. "How often do you do that?"

Mike paused and looked down to the floor. His eyes began to water, and his shoulders slumped. He struggled to keep his composure. "I made a promise to myself after my mother's death, that I would do this in her memory," he said, barely audible. "What started off as an obligation, born from the guilt of not spending enough time with my mother in her final years, is now a source of great joy for me."

I wasn't sure what to say, so I chose to say nothing and let him continue.

"I come in once a week for a few hours," continued Mike. "It really is a small gesture that gives me great joy."

"I appreciate the sharing of the experience," I replied. "It has caused me to evaluate my own contributions to the community—or lack thereof."

"Don't be too hard on yourself, Don," replied Mike. "It took me a long time to learn this lesson, so I am happy to pay it forward whenever I can."

I nodded and smiled.

"What did you notice about the individuals we met today?" Mike asked as he straightened his posture and ran his hand through his hair.

I wasn't sure how to respond. "On the surface, very pleasant and interesting. They all have a different story to share," I said with some hesitation.

"Indeed," replied Mike. "I brought you here to fully understand that this is where we are all heading."

I questioned, "You mean a retirement home?"

"Not quite," chuckled Mike. "The stage of our life where what matters most is the experiences we have had, the love we have shared, the people in our lives, and the need to be part of a larger community. During the first half of our lives, we are willing to trade our health and our relationships to chase and pursue things. In the latter stages of life, we would gladly trade in our things to gain greater quality of life and better relationships."

"It sounds absurd when you put it in those terms," I said. "But it's exactly what Mary and I have done." I paused to take all this in. The idea of aligning our wealth with our values and leaving the world of fight or flight behind was extremely appealing. "How do Mary and I escape this cycle given the grim picture of the future you have painted?" I asked.

Mike put his hand on my shoulder and said, "Remember *A Tale of Two Cities* by Charles Dickens? 'It was the best of times, it was the worst of times, it was the age of wisdom, it was the age of foolishness, it was the epoch of belief, it was the epoch of incredulity, it was the season of Light, it was the season of Darkness, it was the spring of hope, it was the winter of despair …'"

"I think I understand," I said. "We have the choice to continue to go on blindly or make the necessary changes to prosper."

"Well put, Don," Mike replied. "Let's discuss this in more detail at our next meeting. It's time we shifted to the solution to making it out of the retirement anxiety trap and start building your wealth with purpose. What is headed toward us will be the worst of times for many and the best of times for those who are prepared."

Mike and I parted ways, with him promising as always to e-mail us about our next meeting.

Section 2
The Solution

10

Start with Purpose

Two weeks had gone by since our last meeting with Mike. I had transitioned into my new position as an independent contractor with my former employer. Mary had put all of our important financial documents together, and for the first time in years we had a feeling of being in control of our financial destiny.

Something had happened when I gathered the courage to face our crisis head-on. I was still afraid, but I gained the energy to tackle what was in front of me. My outbursts were few and far between, and I felt fully responsible for my own well-being. No more blaming the world for my life.

Our next meeting with Mike would not take place at Café Milano. Mike invited us to join him at his home. He had sent us an e-mail the day before with the change of plans. Mary and I were both intrigued by the idea of getting to see how Mike and his family lived. Mike had also sent us an e-mail sharing his own personal approach to managing his wealth. Unlike traditional financial planning, which was based on a number of myths, Mike's approach had been tested by over thirty years of building and protecting his family's wealth. Mike's approach was based on three key principles:

1) Having a clear purpose for wealth is the starting point to lasting success and fulfillment.

2) The natural cycle of capitalist economies is boom to bust.

3) Individuals, now more than ever, must take responsibility for their own financial well-being.

I knew by the street address that Mike lived in one of the most affluent neighborhoods in Oakhill. Monster homes had been popping up like mushrooms in the area, and there appeared to be no end to the game of building bigger than your neighbor. As we continued to drive on Madeline Side Road looking for Mike's address, we noticed a white farmhouse adjacent to an enclave of pine trees. It stood out so dramatically because it appeared to be the only original home and looked quite out of place relative to the new mansions. As we approached the white house, we noted a relic of a mailbox with the address 7585 Madeline Avenue. To our surprise, this was Mike's home.

"Well," Mike said as he strolled out his front door, "what do you think of the place?"

"Not quite what I pictured you in," I replied.

Mike laughed, "That's because you have been watching too much HGTV. We are living in the era of the dream house, and it has become part of our culture for sure. In the last thirty years, the average home has almost doubled in square footage, while the average family size has decreased by approximately 50 percent."

"It is a strange phenomenon when you put it into those specific terms," I replied. I surveyed the entire property and noticed several acres of farmland. The closest home was at least two acres from Mike's property.

"I have been approached by several developers to sell at a very substantial profit. But I have no interest in selling," Mike said.

"Why not?" I asked. "Isn't a great investment like this the key to building financial security?"

"Don," Mike said in what I recognized as his serious tone, "the most important things in life are not for sale. This property is the embodiment of our core values and was never purchased as an investment property."

Mike motioned us to walk to the back of the house. We sat under a large oak tree as Mike poured three glasses of water from a pitcher. He reached into his shirt pocket and pulled out a small laminated card. "I carry this with me every day as a reminder. This is a quote from the late Earl Nightingale," he said. "'Success is the progressive realization of a worthy ideal.'"

Mike paused and rubbed his chin as if contemplating how to proceed. "Early in my career, I did everything I could to amass as much money as possible. You could say my sole driving purpose was the accumulation of more. Then one day I woke up with someone on top of me pumping my chest, and realized that everything I had worked so hard to achieve was an illusion. I had lots of stuff but was losing my health and my important relationships. I suffered a severe heart attack that should have killed me on the spot. It sounds like a cliché, but faced with the prospect of losing what really mattered to me, I decided to make sweeping changes."

"I guess you just naturally assume that more is better," Mary said. "It seems that everything in our society can be disposed of or upgraded."

"You're right, Mary," replied Mike. "There has been a massive shift in society in the last thirty years from securing our needs to chasing our wants with reckless abandon. This is why people are maxing out their home lines of credit and their credit cards. There is always something else to want or to chase. Even though we have the highest standard of living compared to the rest of the world, it just never seems to be enough."

"I know that I feel trapped by the lifestyle we have created," I said. "But I am not sure how to get out of this vicious cycle."

Mike replied, "What I have discovered, the hard way, is that in order to find any fulfillment in relation to your finances and your quality of life, you must take a purpose first approach."

"What do you mean by purpose?" inquired Mary.

"When we purchased this property, it was so that we could create a simple, comfortable, and secure lifestyle," Mike said. "Having an open space that we could enjoy was more important than the latest design features and home improvement gadgets. We carefully selected this property based on what was important to us. We made sure that the purchase of this home was in line with our values, as opposed to looking at it from a purely economic gain point of view. "

My thoughts drifted to our new home. I can't even remember why we decided to move from our home of the previous twenty-five years. It seemed like everyone else was doing it and we should do it too. In hindsight, the new home has not brought me any more joy. It was about keeping up with our friends. What we gained in home equity, we gave up in cash flow and lifestyle. As Mike was speaking, it really hit home that we had made a very foolish trade-off.

"I think I understand," Mary said. "Knowing not only what you want, but why you want it."

"Exactly," replied Mike. "What Earl Nightingale referred to as a 'worthy ideal,' I refer to as 'purpose.' Defining the purpose of your wealth is the first step to escaping the retirement anxiety trap. This puts you more at ease, because you know where you want to go and why you want to go there. You will consciously choose your lifestyle instead of simply doing what everyone else is doing. You will earn, use, and share wealth in a manner that reflects your core values. Purpose is the starting point, but you still need a financial engine to get you where you want to be."

"I hate to be skeptical about this, Mike. But it sounds a little too new age or self-help for me. I would rather continue working on cleaning up our finances first," I said.

"Don," Mike said reassuringly, "do you have any idea how many personal finance books have been written in the last twenty years?"

"Not really, but I would guess by our visits to the local bookstore, quite a few," I replied.

"I have no idea either," laughed Mike. "But it has to be somewhere in the thousands. Has all of this wisdom translated into better decision making? Rising debt levels and personal balance sheets in total disarray would not support the idea that people need another investment book. My experience is that when you focus solely on financial strategies, you are attempting to cure the symptoms instead of curing the root cause of those symptoms."

"You believe the root cause of the retirement anxiety trap is that most people are not clear about their purpose and values?" asked Mary.

"Precisely," replied Mike. "If you get clear on what really matters to you and you make decisions based on this framework, you will be better able to seize opportunities and protect yourself from financial risks. If I help you with your finances but you use the decision-making process of your past, you will just end up in the same financial position. Remember the statistics on lottery winners?"

"I guess I am fighting you because, at some level, I still want the easy way out," I admitted.

"The process I will share with you may be easier than you think," Mike said. "At this point, what do you have to lose?"

"Nothing," replied Mary. "In fact, I am intrigued to learn more."

Mike replied, "Confusion between goals and purpose are common, but there are some key distinctions. A goal is something that has a beginning and an end. It can be quantified and measured. A purpose, on the other hand, is an overriding intention to live in a certain way. It gives meaning and clarity and acts as a guidepost to all of your decisions. Purpose is based on defining what you want and determining why you want it. If you don't take the time to define why you want something, you will always be chasing the next more. When you pursue wealth just for the sake of accumulating and spending it, you will constantly sabotage yourself and your retirement."

"That makes sense," Mary replied. "But how do we do this?"

Mike continued, "There are three steps to building your wealth with purpose. They include clarifying your values, choosing your lifestyle, and creating alignment with your finances."

"I think I get it," I said. "Begin with the end in mind, as opposed to chasing the money."

"Yes," said Mike as he poured water into each of the empty glasses. "Clarifying your personal code of values forms a strong foundation for personal growth and financial success. Your personal code of values is what's important to you—not something you want or would like to have, but something you literally need in your life to be true to yourself. A value is a principle or quality intrinsically valuable or desirable to you. Being clear about your personal code of values offers the following benefits: decisions are easier, choices are clearer, and your stress is reduced.

"When you are clear on your values, you will gain the ability to define the type of lifestyle that you truly desire. You will have a framework to make better financial choices, and ultimately you will experience greater peace of mind and more success. For example, in recent conversations you and Mary have indicated your desire to travel more. Yet most of your free cash flow is being used to support a house that is quite likely too big for you. Imagine a series of decisions such as this one compounding to create a lifestyle created by chasing something as opposed to being clear about what you really want.

"Once you are clear on your values and the type of lifestyle you want to create, you will need to determine how much money it will take to fund that lifestyle. As a general rule of thumb, assume that as you enter your retirement years, you will need approximately 60 to 70 percent of your current income. Some will want to retain their full income in retirement, and others will reduce their income needs dramatically (by choice or by necessity). You will need that income to last you at least twenty-five years."

Mike paused and looked at his watch. "Oops, I did not realize that the hour had passed so quickly. I hate to be so abrupt, but I need to get back to the Café."

Mary and I stood up and prepared to walk back to our car with Mike.

"Let me give you a challenging exercise to work on before our next meeting," Mike said. "If you start with your purpose and values, you will have a much clearer picture of what you truly want to accomplish. You may find that you need less capital than you originally thought. You may find that you can simplify your life, reposition your capital, and make more integrated choices. Take your core values, associated lifestyle choices, and funding requirement and place them in the following statement:

The purpose of our wealth is to express our core values of [insert core values] and to create the following lifestyle [insert lifestyle]. In order to accomplish this, we would like to create an annual income of [xxxx].

"Creating a purpose statement is not an exact science. You may also find that you are changing and refining your purpose statement over time. It's important that you start with a defining statement and allow it to grow or change over time."

As we walked toward our car, Mary and I accepted the challenge and said our good-byes. The whole way home, we discussed the meeting with Mike and creating a purpose statement for our wealth.

- 11 -

Align Your Goals with Your Purpose

Two weeks had passed since our last meeting with Mike. With my new career and Mary being offered a full-time position at the bank, we were running on fumes when it came to the challenge Mike had put in front of us. An e-mail from Mike a few days ago informed us that our next meeting would be via teleconference.

"How's it going with the challenge I gave you?" Mike asked, his voice echoing over our speakerphone.

Mary and I were sitting at our kitchen table with pen and paper in hand.

"It's been a struggle," Mary replied.

"I know," said Mike. "Keep plugging away and don't worry about being perfect. By the way, I apologize for not being able to make our meeting. I had to fly out to California for a business meeting but will be back in town next week."

"Thanks, Mike," I replied. "If you don't mind me asking, what are you doing in California?"

"I am taking a tour of a number of Silicon Valley headquarters," beamed Mike through the speakerphone. "Several large technology firms in California have managed to cut their energy consumption by up to 75 percent using green technologies. I am here to see how they did it."

"Fascinating," Mary replied. "It seems as if the movement to green technology is really accelerating."

"It is indeed," replied Mike. "I will share more of my thoughts on how you can benefit from the green infrastructure boom, but first things first. Let's get you clear on where you are today in relation to your wealth and where you would like to be."

As requested by Mike, Mary and I had purchased a retirement planning software program. Unlike traditional retirement planning software, this particular program we purchased had a unique characteristic: it was based on actual stock market history of the past hundred years. From 1901 to 2008, a period of 107 years, there have been twenty-five bear markets, or one on average of every 4.3 years. Those twenty-five bear markets averaged a decline of 36 percent in the broad stock market index. The worst averaged a decline of 50 percent.

The software allowed us to "stress-test" our investment portfolio and how a bear market in stocks might impact our wealth. As we learned from Mike, one of the fundamental failures of the financial advisory industry is to use straight-line compound math to calculate future portfolio values.

"When we used the software you recommended, Mike, we were shocked by the results," I volunteered. "Based on our current lifestyle and our income needs, our retirement was currently in a shortfall position of more than five hundred thousand dollars. This shortfall represented the amount of money we would require in addition to our current savings to produce enough income to fund our existing lifestyle."

"Understood but not surprising," replied Mike. "Most baby boomers are way behind on their retirement funding needs. But what was your solution to this problem?"

I replied, "After the initial shock, we decided it was time to take a hard look at our current lifestyle and see what changes we can make to align with our purpose and values. Mary was wonderful at keeping us focused and on track. We started by looking at our income and all of our expenses. We then reviewed all of our assets and investment statements. We discussed the type of lifestyle we wanted to create for ourselves and stopped there."

"Yes, we definitely have more work to do on this challenge, but I am starting to see the forest from the trees," said Mary.

"That's great," replied Mike. "Don't be too hard on yourselves. It's a process that takes some time and some work."

"We are going to keep plugging away and have something ready for our next chat," I replied.

"Sounds good," replied Mike. "I am back in town next week and will send you an e-mail to connect."

Conviction in the Face of Adversity

After the last conversation with Mike, Mary and I had been struggling, but finding a way to make progress. We were having meaningful and honest conversations about our values and our wealth. It's amazing what we discovered about each other after so many years of marriage.

Mike e-mailed us upon his return from his trip to meet him at his home for our next chat. As we drove toward his house I asked Mary, "How do you feel about our little exercise on purpose and values?"

"It's a different way of looking at things, which has been very helpful for me to better understand myself and also where you are coming from," Mary replied. "How do you feel?"

"The same," I replied. "I can't believe we have not had this conversation before."

As we approached Mike's home, he was standing at the edge of the driveway and motioned for us to drive the car to the back of the house. We followed his directions and parked just outside of a large garage.

"Top of the morning," Mike said. "I wanted to show you my new pool."

With a remote control, Mike opened a large garage door and presented his indoor swimming pool. The smell was different somehow. It struck me that the pungent odor of chlorine was missing.

"Remember my story about my heart attack?" quizzed Mike. "Well, what I didn't tell you is that my father died of a heart attack when I was ten years old. Instead of learning to appreciate the value of life, the experience of losing my father forged in me a need to amass as much money as possible in the shortest period of time. My values were warped by the tragedy. It wasn't until the moment of almost going to the other side that I realized the true lesson."

Mary and I listened intently.

"You can shift your values by choice, or you can wait for a major crisis to do it for you. I had to learn the hard way," continued Mike.

"I think that's what most people do," I said.

"Maybe," replied Mike, "but baby boomers are keenly aware that longevity of life without quality of life is not something to aspire to."

Both Mary and I nodded in agreement.

"This pool is a gift for my health. I take care of my body and my health because it's one of my top values. I also used all the green technology available in the marketplace, including geothermal heating and solar heating," Mike said proudly as he pointed to the wide array of technology surrounding the pool.

"Excuse my bluntness, Mike," I said. "But given the amount of wealth you have amassed over the years, it's easy for you to make these choices. Your wealth has given you freedom."

Even as I was finishing the sentence, I was internally chastising myself. It had been awhile since I allowed my thoughts to pass through my mouth without my brain filter on.

"Don, it may surprise you to know that I live on a defined budget," replied Mike in a calm voice. "I don't just go out and spend on anything I desire in the moment. I make choices just like everyone else. Remember, wealth is all relative. Everyone can spend more than they can afford to at every level of society. My freedom comes from the fact that I have not burdened myself with too much debt or a lifestyle I can't afford. It's about personal responsibility and choice."

"My apologies," I replied. "You're right. Compared to the majority of the global population, Mary and I would be considered wealthy. The fact that we are in too much debt without enough savings is the result of the choices we have made over the past twenty years. We now own this and take full responsibility for our situation."

"It's tremendous that you can admit this, Don," said Mike. "Most baby boomers are living in a state of denial, hoping the stock market and the government will come to their rescue."

Mary said, "Now that we have gotten Don's embarrassing outburst for the day out of the way, can we move on?"

As I looked at Mary and Mike, shrugging my shoulders in surrender, we all shared a laugh.

"Come sit down on the patio and let's have a look at what you have put together in relation to the challenge I gave you," Mike said.

Mary said after sitting down, "This is a list of our top values, not in any specific order. Financial security for our family; financial independence for Don and me; staying healthy and physically active; spending quality time with our children and friends; contributing to worthy charitable causes."

"We believe that we can accomplish all this on an annual income of seventy-five thousand dollars," I said.

"That's interesting," replied Mike. "I think that number is much lower than you had initially indicated that you required to support your lifestyle."

"It is," I replied. "The breakthrough part of this exercise is that we both realized that we have been overspending and undersaving. It was not easy to admit this to each other and come clean about it. Change is not an easy thing."

Mike smiled and said, "The idea that you can continue to borrow from the future to live in the moment is simply not sustainable, and that's why so many baby boomers and their respective retirement plans are in jeopardy. What about your purpose statement?"

"Yes," Mary said as she pulled a piece of paper from her pants pocket and began to read. "In relation to our purpose, we have created the following: We would like to use our wealth to enjoy our life to the fullest, to preserve the quality of life in our retirement years, to help our children have a good start to their financial future, and to share our many blessings with causes that inspire us."

"Excellent," replied Mike. "You have created a clear purpose for your wealth that is not limited to specific financial goals. Financial goals are important but will only be achieved in the context of your purpose and your values. The truth is that most baby boomers want the same thing in the end."

"Despite my initial resistance, this has been a clarifying experience," I replied somberly.

"Now instead of chasing money to create a life, you are going to create your lifestyle first and figure out the best way to fund that lifestyle," Mike said. "This is the opposite of what you are doing now and the opposite of what most people do."

"We spent a lot of time talking about this challenge and realized that we have been creating more anxiety in our lives than we want," Mary replied.

"Exactly," Mike said. "Think about how absurd it is to chase money without any overriding context. You will just end up in that game of more that we talked about. You will never escape the retirement anxiety trap."

"Going through this process has been a lightbulb experience for me," I said. 'If I take a close look at our finances, I can see how most of what we have been working toward does not meet our purpose and our values."

Mike replied, "As Lao Tse, the Taoist philosopher, once said, 'He who knows others is learned. He who knows himself is wise.'"

"Very true," I said. "So how do we take our newfound clarity and continue to make positive changes toward where we would like to be in the future?"

"Let's take a step back and see what we have done up to this point," replied Mike. "You have defined your core values and the purpose of your wealth. You have created a clear financial picture of where you are today in relation to your net worth and your net cash flow. You have defined your lifestyle and how much it will take to fund your lifestyle. You have also identified your potential retirement shortfall."

"Wow," Mary replied. "I guess we have accomplished quite a bit. I can't describe how much better we feel even though our circumstances have not changed that much."

"Totally agree with that," I added. "While I still fret about our circumstances, at least we know where we stand today and where we want to be."

Mike smiled. "Congratulations on the progress so far. Recognizing the small steps toward your destination helps keep you focused, grounded, and motivated to moving forward."

"How do we retain this positive momentum?" I asked.

"Create a series of goals and take small steps to achieving those goals," Mike replied. "Goals are an important element to helping you fulfill the purpose of your wealth. Goals help define your actions and provide you with a form of feedback. Dr. Maxwell Maltz, author of *Psycho-Cybernetics*, wrote that 'human beings have a built-in goal-seeking "success mechanism" that is part of their subconscious mind.' According to Dr. Maltz, when your target is vague or not defined, your success mechanism can become confused and unfocused."

"We can definitely benefit from more focus," I said. "Can you elaborate on a goal-setting process?"

"Sure," replied Mike. "The first step is to make your goal specific and measurable. The second step is to ensure that this goal is attainable. That doesn't mean that it has to be easy. Effective attainable goals are reachable, but the reach should cause you to have to expend some effort. Every goal should cause you to stretch outside of your comfort zone to achieve. You should feel as if all of your goals are attainable, but they should also require your full effort and dedication. The third step is to prioritize with a timeline. It can be whenever you want, as long as you have a realistic and attainable deadline to work with. Timelines and prioritization are important components to the science of goal achievement."

"I think we can do that," replied Mary. "But what happens if we don't achieve what we want? How do we keep from getting disappointed and giving up?"

"Excellent question, Mary," Mike replied. "Soon after you set your goals, something you didn't expect may happen to halt your forward momentum. Recognize that obstacles, setbacks, and challenges are inevitable. Just as important as the goal itself is the progress and the journey you make toward the goal. The more you can honor the small steps, the more likely you are to remain focused on completing the goal."

We left the meeting with Mike with a number of goals in mind. We talked about each of our individual goals and then moved to our collective goals during the drive home. We were looking forward to coming up with our goal list.

Supersize Your Savings

"It's great to be back in the land of coffee and croissants," I said as I strolled into Café Milano two weeks following our tour of Mike's state-of-the-art swimming pool.

"Welcome back," Mike said, looking up from reading the newspaper.

"We have had some major breakthroughs this week and are keen to share," Mary said enthusiastically.

"Please do," replied Mike as he motioned for us to sit down with him.

"We brought you a gift," Mary said as we sat down. She handed Mike a large tray filled with cookies.

"Wow," said Mike. "These smell great! What are they?"

"I am teaching a baking class at the local women's shelter," Mary said. "This is our latest project: organic, fair-trade cocoa and coconut cookies."

"That's amazing," said Mike as he reached over to touch Mary's arm.

"Not only is the class part of a self-esteem program, but we are also selling the cookies to raise money and awareness for the shelter," Mary said.

"Well, I would love to showcase these cookies in our store," said Mike after sampling two of them. "They taste fantastic and will sell very well."

"We have another surprise for you," I said. "Based on a thorough review of our finances, we know that we need to spend less and save a good deal more. Although we always intuitively felt this, we were not being honest about our situation. We have decided that our first major step toward solving this problem is to sell our house."

Mike paused before replying, "But you purchased this as your dream home."

Mary said, "We know that we overcommitted to buy the home, and we also know that we can continue to overspend on the house or focus on our purpose and our values. There is no guarantee that our house will continue to rise in value, and there is certainly no guarantee that mortgage interest rates will remain low enough for us to meet our retirement plans. This way we will be completely debt-free and eliminate all of our credit card balances."

"This must have been a tough decision," Mike said sympathetically.

"To be honest, Mike, it wasn't," I replied. "Once we got clear on our purpose and our values, this just made practical sense. We figure we can add over three hundred thousand dollars to our investment portfolio by selling our home and purchasing a new place. We can also free ourselves from our endless house projects and maintenance costs. The financial pressure goes way down, and we get to live the lifestyle that's important to us."

"Congratulations to both of you," Mike said. "Many people would look at this as a failure in the current era of the 'dream home,' but you have made a clear decision based on what's important to you."

"I feel twenty pounds lighter," I joked.

"What you have realized is that you need to save more and spend less," Mike said as he poured each of us a cup of freshly brewed coffee. "I call this supersizing your savings. The average baby boomers can easily cut 5 percent of their expenses and increase their personal savings rate by 5 percent, creating a surplus to pay down debt or increase their retirement assets."

"It's a more manageable and sound approach," Mary said in her pragmatic tone. "We have been cutting back on discretionary spending and have noticed that we are building more momentum as we go along. The savings become contagious."

"Savings are the foundation for long-term personal gain and real wealth accumulation," continued Mike. "Do you remember when a credit card was for convenience, not a reason to buy things that we could not afford?"

"But isn't a high savings rate bad for the economy overall?" I chimed in with some recent insights I had gained from my research into the capital booms and busts of the last four hundred years. "I mean, look at Japan in the 1990s. Personal saving rates skyrocketed to more than 15 percent, and their economy has been in a perpetual on and off recessionary cycle."

"Bravo, Don!" exclaimed Mike. "That is a very good point. John Maynard Keynes, the economist, referred to this as the *'paradox of thrift.'* What is good for the individual—a higher savings rate—can be damaging to the economy. However, an economy that relies on excessive consumer spending to maintain higher growth rates is not sustainable."

"So our gain is the economy's loss?" I asked hesitantly.

"In the short term, yes," replied Mike. "But remember, part of my philosophy is that you as an individual are responsible for your future and no one is coming to your rescue. In this regard, you will have to manage your wealth in a different manner to ensure your financial security. In the long run, a high personal savings rate can be very good for an economy."

As we wrapped up our talk, Mike walked up to the main counter, picked up a flyer, and handed it to us. The flyer included the meeting time and location for our next meeting.

- 13 -

Consume Consciously

As an independent contractor, I found life definitely more hectic. I was travelling much more than I liked, but I knew that this was a temporary situation. Both Mary and I were relishing our new approach to building our wealth with purpose. Almost a month had gone by since our last meeting with Mike, and we were anxious to keep moving to the next level of knowledge and action. We held the flyer that Mike had given us as we made our way to the local fairgrounds, which was hosting a new event that was making its rounds across our state.

"Can you smell it?" Mike asked, standing beside the entry gates to the fairgrounds as he took a deep breath in and exhaled loudly.

Not sure what to smell for, we walked with Mike past the main entry gates. There was a bustling of activity and commerce taking place all around us.

"It's the smell of freshness and life," Mike said. "This is *conscious consumption* in its full glory and energy."

"Conscious what?" I queried. It was a challenge to keep up with Mike's terminology.

"That's right, Don," replied Mike as he put his arm around my shoulder and led us to a booth of locally grown produce. "The past twenty years have been about overspending, overleveraging, and buying everything from the global marketplace. The next twenty years will be about saving more, sourcing locally, and spending by combining your pocketbook and your social conscience."

"So the era of globalization is coming to an end?" asked Mary.

"No, not in the least," replied Mike, sensing our confusion. "Globalization is here to stay, but you and I will start to spend our money in a way that matches our values and also recognizes the value of locally grown food and locally produced products and services. There will also be a movement to buy the products and services of those organizations that are living up to their social and environmental obligations."

"I see," replied Mary. "Globalization continues but in a more balanced manner."

"That's exactly right, Mary," Mike said as he paid for seven apples at the organic produce booth. "Some parts of our consumption experience will remain in the realm of globalization, while others will become more local. This will happen because of changes in energy prices, changes in consumer demand, and changes in the demands we make on the companies we buy from to better manage their impact on society."

"Are you referring to the organic and fair-trade movements?" asked Mary.

"Yes, but much more than that," replied Mike as he handed Mary and me each an apple. "Conscious consumption is about waking up to the impact you have on the world around you with every dollar you choose to spend."

"So it's like waking up to your life and being present with your spending choices on a daily basis?" quizzed Mary.

As Mike and Mary continued their lively discussion, I was surprised to take notice of so many services that I had never been aware of. Everything from locally grown produce to clothing made out of plant-based materials. It was a representation of the best ideas and products for a sustainable world. What was even more surprising was the number of individuals in attendance.

"While all of this is impressive, perhaps it's a little naïve to think we can make much of a difference," I said. "After all, there are more than six billion people who need to be part of the solution."

Not fazed by my comment, Mike continued, "Perhaps, Don. But if we all took that position, then labor laws, environmental concerns, and societal concerns will always take a backseat to instant riches. The truth is that we can all make small changes that will have a large combined and cumulative impact. I am not advocating that we trade in everything for loincloths. Nor am I interested in dismantling capitalism and the benefits of corporate profits."

"You believe that there can be a harmonious balance," Mary said, finishing Mike's thought.

"Exactly," replied Mike. "Corporations and governments will eventually bow to the will of the people. If we demand it, they will provide it—or else we simply shift our spending dollars and our votes. Democracy works best when the people fully exercise their will. As we make conscious choices about how we spend our money, the marketplace will move to fulfill those choices. This is already happening all around us."

"I think the idea of making small change along the way is doable," I said. "I don't know if every purchase I make can live up to these standards, though."

"Small incremental changes by the many leads to huge changes for all," replied Mike. "Conscious consumption includes two distinct elements. The first is deciding how much of your money you will save and how much you will spend. Your personal savings rate should be approximately 15 percent of your income after taxes. Small changes in your spending and savings habits can create opportunities for the accumulation of wealth over time."

"We are on the way there," Mary said. 'It was hard to start, but the momentum has kicked in. What is the second element?"

Mike replied, "The second element of conscious consumption is aligning your pocketbook with your values and societal concerns. Examples are choosing fair trade, organic, and locally grown. You can also look to those organizations that support your societal and ethical values, including fair labor practices, commitment to a green economy, and reinvestment back into local communities. Each of us will have a slightly different focus on which values are more important than others. As each consumer makes small and incremental changes, the results and benefits for both the individual and society will accumulate over time.

"Many global corporations have come under intense scrutiny and have changed their labor practices, their manufacturing practices, and how they offer products and services to consumers. There can be no greater example of this than North American automobile manufacturers, who have been slow to adopt green technologies. Given the strong demand for consumers to shift away from gas-guzzling SUVs to more fuel-efficient models, the

North American automobile industry faces its biggest challenge in its hundred-year history."

"In a nutshell, we can choose to reward those companies that give us products and services aligned with our core values and penalize the ones that don't," I said.

"Yes," agreed Mike. "While it may be a challenge to practice this with every single purchase we make on a daily basis, we can choose to make more conscious choices than we have made in the past. In this way, we begin to integrate our core values into our consumption on a daily basis, and we create positive momentum. The power we have as consumers carries with it great potential and great responsibility. For organizations, both local and global, the choice is very simple: give consumers what they want, when they want it, or go bankrupt. The condition to earn our spending dollars is to align their business practices and their products and services with our values."

As we walked around the fairgrounds, I became increasingly aware that all these people around me were looking for a change to the status quo. Human ingenuity and the will to make progress were evident in every booth and in every financial transaction. It also dawned on me that it was the first time in my life that I was able to see the world through a glass that was half full, rather than half empty.

We thanked Mike for the novel location of our meeting and spent the rest of the day wandering about the fairgrounds.

Yield and Allocate Your Way to Wealth

Three weeks had gone by since our meeting with Mike at the fairgrounds. At Mike's suggestion during our last meeting, Mary and I kept a record of the money we spent on a daily basis and where that money was going. In many ways, this experience was like waking up to our life as opposed to running on autopilot. The fact that we were able to bring our habits into the light provided us with the opportunity to change and shift those habits.

We decided to ride our new bikes to Café Milano to meet with Mike. The bikes were part of our commitment to exercise and health.

"Up here, guys," yelled Mike from atop the rooftop of Café Milano. Both Mary and I were startled by Mike's yelp. We could see Mike peering over the ledge with his boyish enthusiasm.

"What are you doing up there?" I asked.

"Just checking out our new solar panel installation," shouted Mike. "Have a seat, and I will join you in a minute."

Mary and I waited patiently for Mike to come down from the roof. I could not help but think aloud that Café Milano was simply too small to hold Mike's energy and passion.

"So it's now official," chimed Mike as he burst through the front door full of energy and excitement. "Café Milano is now proudly producing green energy."

"That's great," Mary replied. "Now you just need to get the rest of the world to follow suit."

"It's in progress, Mary," replied Mike. "Perhaps more slowly than we want, but remember my comments on momentum. The momentum has shifted to green energy, and the solution is through the capital system, not around it. Think 'green boom.' But before we get any further, tell me about your few weeks of conscious consumption."

"Enlightening," Mary replied.

"One of the great lessons from my Zen training is to live in the moment fully and completely," Mike said. "This is what you experienced by keeping a journal of your expenditures."

"Not only was the exercise clarifying, but we identified at least two hundred dollars per month of unnecessary spending," I said. "Over a ten-year period, this is more than twenty thousand dollars, not including any growth on these savings."

Mike chuckled, "Wow, Don, you're talking like a true contrarian these days. Now that you are on your way to growing your savings pool and aligning your spending with your values, let me share the investment philosophy that will save your retirement from disaster in the next decade."

Before he continued, Mike dashed behind the main serving counter and came back with a white envelope in hand. "Before I forget, I wanted to give you this," he said.

Mary took the envelope in her hand and opened it.

"Wow," she exclaimed. "Are you kidding me?"

"Not one bit," replied Mike.

"What is it?" I asked, peering over Mary's shoulder.

"It's a check for your first batch and an order for five hundred cookies," Mike replied.

Mary could not contain her excitement. "The women at the shelter are going to be thrilled."

"Congratulations on your hard work, Mary," said Mike. "Now, let's get back to Don and his comment about growing your wealth."

I planted a big kiss on Mary's cheek. I reminded myself to tell her more often how much I appreciated her.

Mike continued, "There is a wonderful old truism that is shared as an inside joke among Wall Street traders. It goes something like this: 'Speculation is an effort to turn a little money into a lot. Investment is an effort to prevent a lot of money becoming a little.' By far the biggest mistake investors, and the majority of financial advisors, make is that they confuse investing with speculating. The fundamental difference is that speculating involves making decisions solely on the basis that their investment will appreciate in value over time. It's a one-sided interpretation of a complex financial decision. Think about how individuals have been speculating in housing values in the past decade. As we can clearly see with the most recent housing downturn, choosing solely to chase a rising price can be very dangerous."

"So if you are investing solely because you think prices are going to go higher, this is dangerous?" I asked.

"Yes, as my friend the professor clearly demonstrated, the stock market and the real estate market do not move up in a straight line," replied Mike. "There have been many periods of considerable lengths of time during the past one hundred years where both the stock market and the real estate market have not appreciated in value. Betting on capital appreciation has not guaranteed your success."

"So if we can't expect the stock market or real estate market to go up in value, what do we do?" asked Mary.

"A more successful approach to investing is to ensure that you are getting paid to wait for capital appreciation," replied Mike. "This is why the concept of yield is so important."

"I see," Mary replied. "This is a far cry from our current portfolio strategy. We go up and down with the markets like the proverbial yo-yo and don't seem to be any further ahead in the past ten years."

"Exactly," replied Mike. "When it comes to getting paid to wait, let's explore both the stock market and the real estate market. Research proves that over time, it's better to invest in stocks that pay you a dividend than those that do not. A dividend is the sharing of the corporations' profits and can either be taken as income or reinvested to purchase more of the companies' shares. The amount of money that is paid as a dividend relative to the price of the stock is referred to as the *dividend yield*. A yield can provide you with income or some downward protection in a volatile and choppy market."

"That's how my dad used to invest," I commented. "If a stock did not have a good dividend attached to it, my dad would not invest in it. While not politically correct, my dad used to say that this was the 'widows and orphans' approach to investing."

"I agree that this would not be a politically correct term for today's world," said Mike. "That's why I refer to this investing approach as going back to the 1950s. That generation of investors was more cautious and risk averse. They wanted to get paid to wait and did not trust that stock prices would simply rise every year. But what your dad was essentially saying was that if a company could afford a good dividend, it offered the extra safety of being paid to wait for growth. Most individuals have forgotten this truism."

"I know we have," Mary replied. "The financial industry mantra of buy and hold has not worked for us …"

"Totally understandable," replied Mike. "The financial advisory business is a by-product of the financial expansion of the last twenty-five years. Investing for growth has worked for so long that advisors and investors forgot that stock markets can decline in dramatic fashion. The notion of getting paid to wait for growth will come back into fashion in the coming decade as investors realize that the stock market does not always go up."

"I understand how this applies to our stocks, but what about a real estate investment?" asked Mary.

Mike replied, "In terms of investing in real estate, outside of your principal residence, the same mistake was made by most baby boomers. Let's use the example of purchasing a rental property as part of your overall portfolio. The rent that you generate from the property compared to whatever you pay for the property is referred to as the *gross yield*. However, gross yield can be misleading because it does not factor in all of your expenses, such as mortgage interest, property taxes, maintenance, and utilities. That is why the concept of a *net yield* is more relevant for investing in real estate. You can think of this as the *dividend ratio* for a rental property. You should be able to readily calculate your return after all expenses have been paid, without factoring in capital appreciation. If you cannot earn a positive *net yield* and put money in your pocket every month, does it make sense to solely speculate on a rising asset value? My belief is that the answer is no. Just like in the stock market, real estate is subject to the ebbs and flows of economic cycles. You would much prefer that your investment paid you a certain positive amount every month."

"It's funny how it makes so much sense, and yet all of us have been chasing rising asset values in both the stock market and the real estate market," Mary said.

"Exactly, Mary," replied Mike. "History tells us that both the real estate and stock market can experience periods lasting up to twenty years where there is very little capital appreciation. Most baby boomers cannot afford to wait twenty years for their investment to appreciate in value. They need to think in terms of getting paid to wait."

"How much we pay for an investment and what it can generate for us as an income is very important," I said. "But what about the timing of our investment decisions in respect to both bull and bear markets in real estate and stocks?"

"Great point," replied Mike as he stood up to grab three glasses of water for us. "When yields begin to compress below their long-term averages, both in the stock market and real estate, it is an indication that asset values are appreciating above their long-term averages. This means that investors are willing to pay higher and higher prices in the pursuit of capital gains. This happens both in real estate and in the stock market. I would suggest that is an opportune time to rebalance your holdings and wait for corrections and buying opportunities. In recent years, yields on real estate investments and stocks have shrunk to less than 2 percent per annum. That means you could earn more in a treasury bill with no risk. The compression of investment yields is an important metric in helping you make good investment decisions. Remember, capital appreciation is never a guaranteed outcome either for real estate or the stock market."

Mary said, "The notion that an investment will appreciate in value over a specific period of time is one of the financial planning myths we have to be wary of."

"Exactly," replied Mike with a smile. "But I must give you the exception to this. In terms of real estate, stocks, and bonds, a relatively high yield may indicate that investors believe the following: 1) that the underlying investment is of higher risk, and 2) that future income streams associated with the investment may be reduced."

At this point I was confused, and I could tell Mary was struggling as well. "So, both very high yields and very low yields may indicate that the underlying investment is risk?" I asked.

"There is a certain contradiction here," replied Mike. "And that's why you should not use the metric of yield as the lone decision-making factor when building your investment portfolio," replied Mike. "You need to look at yield in the context of building a diversified portfolio and managing your investment risk."

"So, taking this all in, how do we build a *yield-driven portfolio* that takes investment risk into account?" asked Mary.

As part of our preparation for our next meeting, Mike asked us to do some research on what he referred to as a "core and explore investment strategy." Mary and I decided to tackle this together. Our next meeting was to take place at a condominium tower just north of Café Milano, in suite 444.

Go Core and Explore

"Why do you think we are meeting here?" I asked Mary as I rang the doorbell to suite 444.

"Your guess is as good as mine," Mary replied. "But I am sure Mike will have some kind of surprise waiting for us."

"Good afternoon, Don and Mary," Mike said, answering the door in a pair of scruffy-looking overall pants that were spattered with paint. "Welcome to one of my local rental units that is currently getting a facelift."

"You own this condominium?" I asked.

"Oh yes, and many more," exclaimed Mike. "I love to own real estate that pays me on a monthly basis. Whether this condo goes up in value or not, I get paid. Over the long term, my rental income pays off my mortgage balance, and I build a large pool of equity. I bought this real estate investment using the yield approach I shared with you."

"Can you elaborate?" I asked.

"I first selected what I thought was a reasonable return on my capital, assuming that this property would not appreciate in value and might actually go down by 30 percent," Mike said.

"Very conservative," responded Mary. "Taking a potential loss of that magnitude into account is something very new to us. It makes sense to plan for both the best and worst outcomes."

"Agreed," replied Mike. "I studied condominium prices in the area that would support my required return based on a down payment of 50 percent. I wanted to keep my leverage in line with my worst-case scenario. Finally I looked at average rents in the area to make sure I would be in a positive cash flow from day one of my investment. That screening process narrowed my choices down to about twenty properties. I hired a very knowledgeable real estate agent to help me finish my due diligence, and voila," finished Mike, raising his arms at his sides.

Fascinated by Mike's analysis and also encouraged that we could duplicate his process and results, I asked, "So, real estate is a major part of your holdings?"

"No," replied Mike, much to our surprise. "Real estate is part of my overall asset allocation strategy. It is simply one of the asset classes that make up my overall portfolio."

As we moved into the center of the condo unit, Mike pointed over to a bare table and three chairs. "Please, have a seat. This is a good segue into the topic I want to share with you today—the *core and explore* approach to investing."

"We have done quite a bit of work on this topic, based on the guidance you provided, and have learned a great deal in the process," I said. "Mary will provide the summary of our research."

Mary started by clearing her throat, "A core and explore approach to investing can generally be defined as moving the bulk of your portfolio to asset classes that are more conservative in nature and do not require a lot of your effort to manage. Such investments in the core section of your portfolio may include cash, treasury bills, and government bonds. The rest of your portfolio, or what can be referred to as the explore portion, should be allocated to higher-risk investments, such as corporate bonds, equities, real estate, and sector-specific investments."

"That's right," Mike said. "The notion behind the core and explore approach is that you build a portfolio that is focused on managing your investment risk as well as generating investment performance. The core and explore approach is used effectively by large pension funds and endowment funds. Individual investors often focus on chasing higher values without taking into account the risk they are taking."

As Mary wrapped up her notes, I looked over to Mike and said, "I can see how we have totally invested the wrong way over the past ten years. We have been overexposed to equities and have been too aggressive."

"Well, that's true of most individuals," replied Mike. "Returns are relevant only in the context of the risk you are taking to earn them. Unfortunately most individuals don't understand this until there is a deep decline in stock market values or real estate values."

"So, how do we combine your philosophy of yield with core and explore?" asked Mary.

"Great question," replied Mike. "Let me answer by first explaining the importance of the rate of return variance for a specific portfolio. Studies conducted over the past thirty years of institutional portfolios and pension funds illustrate that up to 94 percent of the variation in investment returns can be attributed to the combination of different asset classes in the portfolios. The remaining variation is attributable to security selection and the timing of purchases and sales."

"So if we want to protect our nest egg and manage our risk, we need to choose the correct asset allocation?" asked Mary.

"That's correct," replied Mike.

"Does this not contradict all the pundits in the media and experts who want you to time the market or pick the best investments at any given time?" asked Mary. "We now have twenty-four-hour television and instant access to every financial guru imaginable."

"Both the media and financial institutions thrive on confusion. The more confused you are, then the more you need what they are selling," replied Mike. The proof is in the independent research."

I was feeling overwhelmed again. "How do we determine the best *asset allocation* strategy for our portfolio? And how do we bring together yield, core and explore, and your comments on portfolio variance?" I asked while shrugging my shoulders.

Mike replied in his reassuring manner, "It really depends on your expectations of what the economy and financial markets will do over the course of the coming decade and how much risk you are willing to take with your investments. Returns and risk must be analyzed as part of an overall decision. As you may have guessed, my personal view is that the perfect financial storm is on its way, and this will lead to a decade of below-average economic growth. The period from the year 2000 to 2010 is now referred to as the 'lost decade' since there was no growth in the stock market over that period. I believe the coming decade will bring more of the same."

"So, how does one best protect and grow their wealth if both the economy and stock market may experience another lost decade?" asked Mary.

"If you have some time, would you like to join me for a quick trip to the cafe?" said Mike. "I can drive, and we can talk more in the car."

Mike quickly changed into a pair of shorts and a polo shirt and directed us to the elevator.

"Are we taking the French fry express?" I asked, hoping the answer was yes.

Mike laughed as the elevator door closed behind us and replied, "You bet."

Somewhat hesitant to intrude on his personal business, I decided to make my request and asked, "Can you show us how to convert our car like you have done with your SUV?"

"Of course," replied Mike as the elevator doors opened and we made our way to Mike's truck. "I was actually wondering why you had not asked before. Besides the green benefits, you are going to be saving money by converting. It's a lot simpler than you might imagine."

"Then why aren't more people making the change?" Mary quizzed.

Mike replied," It's what Malcolm Gladwell, the journalist and author, refers to as the tipping point, Mary. Not enough consumer demand exists to push the technology toward mass consumption. North Americans are spoiled by cheap oil and gas. When an energy crisis hits and enough consumers demand it, change will come. In the meantime, you can enjoy the rewards of being a first mover."

Mike started the truck, and we were immediately immersed in that smell I was growing used to of cooking oil and French fries."

Mike said, "Most individuals start their investment plans the same way. They take on too much risk in hot financial markets and then completely change their approach in poor financial markets. They don't allow enough time for their investments to perform because they made the wrong investment choices to begin with. Most financial advisors are guilty of the same offense. To meet the demands of their clients, they chase performance in frothy financial markets and switch their philosophy when the markets underperform. A financial advisor with a constantly changing philosophy can be very dangerous for your retirement."

Mary and I looked at each other and nodded in agreement.

Mike continued, "A better approach is to determine how much risk you are willing to take to generate your returns and select the 'strategic asset allocation' that best reflects your risk tolerance. Baby boomers need to focus on preserving their wealth during the coming decade of financial crisis. In this regard, I believe you need to be very conservative when choosing your strategic asset allocation."

Mary replied, "Conservative to our previous advisor was to have us buy a basket of mutual funds and stocks and diversify globally. This did not work very well, and we know that we took on way too much risk."

I opened the window in the backseat to let in some fresh air.

"Agreed," replied Mike. "When a true financial crisis hits, most investments, including stocks and real estate both domestic and international, go down at the same time. In the new global world, there is more correlation of investments and asset classes both on the upside and the downside."

I was beginning to grasp Mike's concept of measuring risk in a much broader context. I asked, "So where does one effectively hide out to preserve capital in a financial crisis and also find opportunities to build wealth?"

Mike smiled and replied, "Don, you are really developing a knack for asking the proverbial million-dollar question."

I smiled and mentally patted myself on the back. It felt good to keep up with Mike.

Mike continued, "For the past thirty years, debt has been 'king.' In the coming decade, cash will regain its rightful throne as the new, old king."

Mary asked, "You mean paper over plastic?"

"No," replied Mike. "I mean that in a financial crisis with its roots in deleveraging and deflation, you want to have as little debt as possible and have most of your savings in safe, secure cash investments, with a sprinkling of hard assets and a dash of option instruments."

We arrived at Café Milano more quickly than I expected and followed Mike through the front door. He appeared to be in a rush and moved quickly into the back room; he came back with a yellow notepad and a can of paint.

"I forgot both of these this morning," he said. "The notepad is for you, and the can of paint is for me. Have a look at some notes I put together for you. What you are looking at is my portfolio asset allocation. It's a portfolio put together using the main principles we have discussed up to this point. The proportion that you will allocate to each of these asset classes will depend on your financial objectives and risk tolerance."

I took the notepad and placed it on the table. Mary suggested that she read the material aloud, and I thought that was a good suggestion.

Portfolio Summary

Core

1. *Cash and Short-Term Treasury Bills (T-Bills)* – 60%

These are short-term government obligations, of ninety days or more in term, sold at a discount from face value. Treasury bills generally are issued with maturities ranging from ninety days to two years. They are considered as low-risk investments with lower return potential. They are used to preserve capital and for liquidity. These investments are often covered by federal government deposit insurance.

2. *Stocks/Equities* – 15%

For the purposes of this discussion, the term stock represents the shares of a publicly traded corporation. A stock can create returns in one of two ways. An investor can sell the shares of the company if the company's value per share has increased; or the company can pay dividends, which are earnings that the particular company has elected to distribute to its shareholders. The two broad classes of stock are common stock and preferred stock.

Common Stock

Common stock is a class of stock that has no preference to dividends or any distribution of assets. Common stock usually conveys voting rights to the holder of the stock. Common stockholders are the residual owners of a corporation in that they have a claim to what remains after every other party has been paid. The value of their claim depends on the success of the underlying corporation. Common stock can be domestic or foreign.

Preferred Stock

Preferred stock is a class of stock that provides ownership in a corporation and that gives the holder a claim prior to the claim of common stockholders on earnings and also generally on assets in the event of liquidation. The majority of preferred stock issues pay a fixed dividend set at the time of issuance, stated in a dollar amount or as a percentage of par value. Because no maturity date is stipulated, these securities are priced on dividend yield and trade much like long-term corporate bonds. Their benefits are often misunderstood and not well utilized. This is because most investors are chasing capital gains as opposed to getting paid to wait.

Explore

3. *Corporate Bonds* – 5%

These are bonds issued by corporations that are backed by the balance sheets and business operations of these corporations. Depending on the risk associated with a particular corporation, they may have a higher interest rate attached to them. You should focus on corporations with strong balance sheets that have consistently met their financial obligations. Corporate bonds offer a higher yield than cash and treasuries but come with higher risk. That's why they are included in the explore section of my portfolio.

4. *Covered Call Options* – 10%

Covered Call Option Writing is an option strategy where an investor holds a stock or an index and *writes (sells) call options* on that same asset in an attempt to generate increased income from the asset. When utilizing this option strategy, the investor is neutral to bullish about the direction a stock or a particular index will move in the near term. This option strategy is considered more conservative than strictly buying and holding a stock or an index because the risk is offset by the premium earned for selling the option, known as the "call."

Using this option strategy, the owner of the underlying stock or index is considered the option seller, the "writer." As the writer, the investor is willing to limit the upside potential movement in the stock price or index by selling the option strike price and immediately receiving the option premium that is paid by the option buyer. The writer of the call is then obligated to sell the underlying stock should the stock price move above the option strike price.

No matter what happens to the stock price during the option period, the writer retains the call option premium. If the stock price drops or stays the same through the option period, the stock owner retains the premium and the underlying stock. If the stock price should move above the call option strike price, the writer retains the premium and may have the stock called away by the option buyer. However, the writer realizes profit from the premium and the increase in the stock price minus the stock purchase price. In addition to regular dividends, the premium earned by writing the option can increase the yield for a stock or underlying index.

Buy-write strategies are often used to reduce volatility under certain market conditions, as well as provide additional income to a portfolio through call option premiums. In down markets, for example, the option premiums received mitigate the price decline in an equity portfolio. The trade-off is that in strong equity markets, the upside potential of the equity investment is reduced as the option is exercised above the strike price.

You can also purchase a *"Buy-Write Index,"* which provides a passive approach to using a covered call strategy on a broad stock market index.

5. Gold – 10%

Investment in gold can be done through ownership of physical gold bullion, shares of gold mining companies, or through an index that tracks the price of gold. Gold is considered the ultimate portfolio hedge in volatile times. Specifically, gold is viewed as a hedge against inflation and the devaluation of financial currencies. Consider its use as disaster insurance for your portfolio.

The *Dow/Gold ratio* is the ratio of the price of the Dow Jones to the price of gold. The ratio measures the number of ounces of gold it takes to buy one share of the Dow Jones. For example, with the Dow at 12,000 and gold at 600, it requires 20 ounces of gold to buy one share of the Dow. The ratio, over time, measures the cyclical nature of the value of paper assets (stocks) and hard assets (gold). Stocks excel when everyone believes and is willing to invest in future growth.

When the ratio rises, as it did in the 1920s, 1960s, and 1990s, it tells us that portfolios of stocks should outperform. When the ratio declines, as it did in the 1970s, it indicates that stocks will underperform gold. At the height of each equity bubble over the past one hundred years, the ratio reached in excess of 30 to 1. Since the bursting of the technology bubble, the Dow/Gold ratio has been in steady decline, indicating that gold may continue to be a strong hedge for your portfolio.

"Wow, Mike," I said. "That's a very conservative portfolio. Much more conservative than I would have thought for you."

Mike said, "The main reason I have been able to hold on to my wealth over the years is that I am quite conservative with my core portfolio holdings." As a student of past financial crises, I have a very healthy respect for potentially large and rapid declines in asset values."

"Do you foresee a time when we should be less conservative?" I asked.

"Having a conservative portfolio during a crisis will give you the ability to make good investments when others are forced to sell either through panic or because they do not have enough cash," replied Mike. "Some of the best investments I have made were during periods of financial crisis. However, you don't want to be too early, and you want to make sure you are following your strategic asset allocation at all times."

There was one final strategy documented on Mike's notepad. "What's this *put option strategy* written on your notepad?" I asked.

Mike replied, "It's my stock portfolio insurance plan. If the stock market goes down, the value of my put option goes up and creates a natural hedge or insurance policy for my stock market holdings."

I frowned and said, "That sounds complicated."

Mike replied, "Not really, Don. A put option is a financial contract between two parties, the seller and the buyer of the option. The buyer acquires a short position by purchasing the right to sell the underlying instrument to the seller of the option for a specified price (the strike price) during a specified period of time. If the option buyer exercises their right, the seller is obligated to buy the underlying instrument from them at the agreed upon strike price, regardless of the current market price. In exchange for having this option, the buyer pays the seller a fee (called the option premium). By providing a guaranteed buyer and price for an underlying instrument for a specified period of time, put options offer insurance against excessive loss. The seller of put options profits by selling options that are not exercised. Such is the case when the ongoing market value of the underlying instrument makes the option unnecessary—that is, the market value of the instrument remains above the strike price during the option contract period."

Mary commented, "Like an insurance policy. You are buying insurance on the stock market going down, and the person selling you the insurance is betting that the stock market will not go down."

"Exactly," replied Mike. "I purchase put options on the broader stock market to hedge my stock market holdings. I am not a day trader or options expert, but I find this an effective hedge against significant downturns. If I am wrong, I have lost my insurance premium, which is what I paid for the put option. It's a small risk for a potentially significant insurance policy."

"You have given us a lot to think about," I said. "We are going to have to spend some time with this material before we next meet."

"That sounds good," replied Mike. "Contact me when you're ready to meet again."

- 15 -

Say Good-Bye to Your Mutual Funds

It was almost three weeks since we had last met with Mike. Mary and I were both running at full tilt in our respective jobs, but we made it a priority to set aside a specified time each week to meet and work together to reshape our wealth. It wasn't easy or a quick fix, but it felt good nonetheless.

We had e-mailed Mike a few days prior to meet at our house for lunch. Mary had prepared her special nachos, and I was working on my penne al vodka pasta.

I heard the doorbell and said, "Mary, can you get that? I am in the middle of draining the pasta."

Mary opened the door and greeted Mike with a hug. "It's about time we had you over."

"Yes, that's true," replied Mike. "I am looking forward to lunch."

"Good to see you, Mike," I said wiping the water from my hands on a paper towel. We shook hands, and I patted him on the back as we made our way to the kitchen table.

"I brought you something," said Mike as he removed a strange-looking blue bottle from the paper bag he was carrying. The bottle resembled the shape of a rocket that was bent over on a sixty-degree angle.

"You have to try some of this," Mike said as he asked me to bring three shot glasses to the table. "Let's toast to your progress and to new friends and new beginnings."

As he poured from the bottle into the three glasses I had brought to the table, the liquid that came out of the bottle was transparent and had a very familiar odor. We smacked our glasses together and downed the drinks.

"So, what does a five-hundred-dollar shot of vodka taste like?" Mike asked.

"What!" said Mary, almost choking on her own words. "Are you serious?"

"This rare bottle was a gift from a hedge fund manager back about ten years ago now," Mike said. "I keep it around to remind myself of my greed. You see, I lost about 20 percent of my entire net worth in one really bad investment."

While I was shocked to hear this, I also felt somewhat relieved. Even Mike made mistakes—and big ones too. "The vodka was amazing, but more importantly, how did you lose so much money?" I asked.

"In the late 1990s, I was approached by some people whom I really respected as very bright minds and astute investors to start a new kind of investment fund," replied Mike. "They had come up with a new way to manage money and beat the market. I got greedy and put up a large chunk of my net worth to get them started."

"So you broke your cardinal rule on asset allocation?" asked Mary.

"I thought their approach was bulletproof," replied Mike. "And it was as they produced stellar returns for a short period of time, but then a shift in the Russian currency and interest rates resulted in a collapse of the fund. I did not realize how much debt the managers of the fund had taken on to create the stellar returns. This was my lesson on the risks of too much leverage and greed."

"I remember reading about a massive hedge fund failure in the late 1990s," Mary said. "I would have thought that someone with your insights and talents would not be involved in something like that."

"Well, the greed bug has a way of getting to all of us," Mike said somberly. Mike winked as he poured me another shot of vodka as Mary declined the offer of a second glass. "That was the biggest loss of my investment career. While I thought I knew it all, I learned a valuable lesson: don't try to beat them, own them."

"What do you mean, Mike?" I asked after downing the second shot glass.

Mike continued, "*Active portfolio management* is an attempt to 'beat' the market as measured by a particular benchmark or index. The *Standard*

& Poor's Corp. (S&P) 500 Index is an example of a market index; it tracks the performance of the five hundred largest capitalized stocks in the U.S. stock market. The aim of active management is to outperform a defined index over a particular time frame."

"Don't most active managers underperform their benchmark index?" asked Mary.

"Quite right, Mary," replied Mike. "In fact, recent studies have indicated that up to 90 percent of active money managers underperform their market benchmarks. That's why I am a strong advocate for *passive investment management.* Passive investment management is often referred to as *indexing.* This approach involves investing in exactly the same securities, in the same proportions, as a particular index. Most money managers will not beat the index over a defined period of time, and to add insult to injury, will charge you a management fee for their lack of performance. Why would anyone pay fees of up to 2 percent to a mutual fund manager who will ultimately underperform their benchmark?"

"Agreed," I replied. "But how does this relate to the portfolio examples you provided to us?"

"You have two fundamental choices, after you have defined your strategic asset allocation, to create your portfolio," replied Mike. "You can try to actively manage each component of your portfolio, or you can employ a passive strategy."

"I understand," Mary replied as she removed the nacho platter from the oven and placed it on a heat pad on the kitchen table. "Active money managers believe that they can beat the market, but you don't think this is possible on a consistent basis."

"Exactly right," replied Mike. "The problem is that independent research shows that only a very small percentage of active money managers can make this claim. Since the majority can never beat the market, I would prefer to own the market."

"Dig in," Mary said as she motioned for us to sit and take our serving plates.

"These are fantastic, Mary," beamed Mike. "What flavor and texture!"

"It's the caciocavallo cheese that enhances all the other flavors of the traditional nacho platter," Mary said.

"Yes indeed," replied Mike as he added more nachos to his plate.

"So, you said better to own the market than beat it," I said. "How do we do that?"

"My personal view is that a diversified *ETF portfolio* (exchange traded fund portfolio) is the best way to do this."

"I have been hearing a great deal about exchange traded funds," Mary replied. "Can you elaborate on what they are and how you use them as part of your overall portfolio strategy?"

"I have already explained why I don't believe that individual stock picking is going to work for you," Mike said. "Some of the best stock pickers on Wall Street have a hard time beating their benchmarks, and they work at it almost twenty-four hours per day. What makes an individual investor believe that they will have any more success?"

"I am not sure," I replied. "I guess it's the illusion of instant riches or the emotional rush of speculating on an individual stock."

"Remember that old Wall Street joke about speculating versus investing?" asked Mike rhetorically. "Well, I want you to be investors in long-term capitalism and the prosperity that capitalism offers. No more speculating with the bulk of your wealth."

"How do we do that?" I questioned.

"You do what you have already started to work on," replied Mike. "Build a strategic asset allocation strategy with an emphasis on yield, core, and explore and implement that strategy using ETFs as your primary equity holding."

"What's wrong with mutual funds?" I asked.

"In a nutshell," replied Mike, "their fees are too high, and 90 percent of mutual fund managers will underperform their benchmark. Compounding the problem with mutual funds is that most individuals and advisors buy and sell them at the wrong time because they are trying to time the market."

"But there are managers who do beat the market," I argued.

"Yes," answered Mike. "But they are in the minority, and they do not beat the market every year. They have periods of underperformance and overperformance."

"Can you share some overall thoughts on how you would put this together for yourself?" I asked.

"Of course," replied Mike. "Let me share my ETF Strategy. An ETF is similar to a mutual fund in that it holds a basket of stocks with a unified theme. An ETF, unlike a mutual fund, can be bought and sold like any other equity trading on the stock market. It has a ticker symbol and can be purchased through any discount or full-service broker in the same way you would purchase a stock or a bond. In some ways, it represents the evolution of the mutual fund."

"I see," I replied as I prepared to serve my pasta.

"It's an interesting coincidence, Don," said Mike. "Your pasta dish and my bottle of vodka."

"Yes," I replied. "Except I paid a lot less for mine than you did for yours."

We laughed as we prepared to dig into the pasta.

"Well said and well done, Don," Mike said after trying the pasta. "This is exceptional."

"Thank you," I said. "Before we feel the need to take an afternoon nap from the effects of the vodka, what final pointers can you give us about putting our portfolio together?"

"Of course," said Mike as he picked the last piece of pasta from his plate and wiped his mouth with a napkin. "It's something I wanted to cover but forgot. I call it the cardinal rule of rebalancing."

"That sounds good to me," Mary said. "I don't want to spend my retirement in front of a computer screen. I need something effective and easy."

"Agreed," replied Don. "At the end of every month, I take ten minutes to sit down and review my portfolio. I identify if my strategic asset allocation is in line with my original percentage breakdown and then adjust if required. It takes all the emotions out of my investment decisions."

"Regardless of all the noise and gyration in the stock market, you only take ten minutes each month to rebalance your portfolio?" I asked, both shocked and dismayed.

"That doesn't mean I am not constantly studying trends, opportunities, or dangers," replied Mike. "But I do take a disciplined approach to choosing the right asset allocation for me that will allow me to stay invested in high-quality opportunities. Remember, I also have some insurance protection in place in case the market goes off the rails."

"Yes, I remember this," I said. "I think I get it. Choose the right asset allocation to start, give yourself the time required to make your investments work, and have enough yield and protection to weather the storms."

"Exactly," Mike replied. "It does not mean that you only look at your portfolio once per month, but it does mean that you will be disciplined enough to only make those changes back to your original asset mix that you carefully selected."

We wrapped up lunch with some ice cream and fruit. After Mike left, Mary and I spent the afternoon reviewing our portfolio strategy.

- 16 -

Prepare for Longevity

Two weeks after our vodka-accented lunch with Mike, Mary and I arrived at Café Milano for our next meeting. We sat in our regular seats as Mike greeted us. "Top of the morning," he said, beaming his Broadway smile.

"Good-morning," Mary replied. "We were very curious about the e-mail you sent us a few days ago on the HIPPie dilemma. We thought you might be sharing your stories from Woodstock."

"Hah," Mike replied as he ran his hands through his hair. "I wish I was there for that party."

"And what a party it was," I said, rolling my eyes and shaping my fingers to create the universal "peace sign." "The good old days …"

Mike held up his hands with his palms facing toward us and moved them apart slowly. He had a knack for using exaggerated hand gestures to make his point. It was part of his overall showmanship and charm.

Then he began, "Remember, most baby boomers want to retire earlier and are planning to live longer. This increases the risk of outliving their financial capital. It used to be so easy. Find a good job, get a pension, retire at age sixty-five, and enjoy a good ten years of retirement. A couple now aged sixty-five have a 94 percent chance of one partner living to age eighty and a 63 percent chance of one partner living to age ninety."

"I don't just want a long retirement," I said. "I want to ensure that I am enjoying a high quality of life."

"Of course," replied Mike. "I think we would all like that outcome. But our entire financial and social assistance system was not designed to support this. That's why the risks of outliving your capital are growing every day. It's the *HIPPie* dilemma, *High Income-Pension Poor* baby boomers."

"I can't imagine that anyone who partied at Woodstock could fathom this stage of their life," I said.

"We can relate," Mary said. "But how did we collectively end up in this situation? Did companies and governments see this coming?"

"Well," replied Mike. "Over the past twenty years, corporations have been removing themselves from the pension business. They simply don't want to have the risk of funding retirements. When the average retirement lasted ten years, corporate-funded pension plans were pretty easy to manage. Now the costs to fund a defined-benefit plan have gone through the roof, as based on current mortality rates, an average retirement can last up to twenty-five years. Have you ever noticed that when a public company cuts their pension plan, the value of their stock or shares goes up?"

"I assume you see this as a major trend to continue?" I asked.

"You are right," replied Mike. "The movement away from defined-benefit pension plans is accelerating. What this means in simple terms is that without a good pension plan, baby boomers have a much greater risk of running out of money in their retirement years. They can no longer rely on their employer, and no one I know wants their entire retirement funded by paltry payments from social security. The only solution is personal responsibility, with a small safety net provided by the government."

"What about the portfolio strategy you shared with us?" I asked.

"A good portfolio strategy is one very important arrow in your quiver," replied Mike. "The notion that a portfolio strategy is the end-all and be-all of your retirement planning is not only foolish but actually quite dangerous."

"How so?" I asked.

"One of the myths we talked about in relation to traditional financial planning is too much faith in the stock market and not enough focus on mitigating your risks," Mike said. "It's very disturbing that many financial advisors don't fully understand many of the risk transfer strategies available to individual investors."

"The concept of transferring some of our risks is very appealing," Mary commented.

"Agreed," replied Mike. "A holistic approach to dealing with the HIPPie dilemma is to have a number of elements integrated into your financial affairs designed to either mitigate your risks or transfer them. There is a cost to do this, but the cost must be viewed in relation to the benefits gained.

"There are many strategies available to investors to transfer some of their retirement risks. The concept of transferring risk is quite simple. For a specified fee, you can choose to transfer some or the bulk of your risks to a financial institution. In every transaction, there is a cost and a benefit. You must be aware of both. The two risk transfer strategies that are most relevant for baby boomers are *annuities* and *variable annuities*.

"How do they work?" asked Mary.

"Let me get you a coffee while I answer that," Mike said.

"Can you use just one sugar, Mike?" I asked.

Mike nodded as he said, "An annuity is an investment that pays you a set monthly income for a set period of time. With an annuity, you agree to pay an insurance company a lump sum of money up front, and they in turn agree to return to you a set monthly income for a defined term or the rest of your life. The income stream will vary with your age, your health, and prevailing interest rates at the time. The primary use of annuities is to ensure that you will not outlive your capital. The main disadvantage to the annuity is that you are giving up control of your capital in return for a defined income stream."

"So you might say that is part of an overall investment strategy and has a specific use?" asked Mary.

"Well put, Mary," replied Mike as he came back to the table with our coffees. "A variable annuity is a contract between you and an insurance company under which you make a lump-sum payment or series of payments. In return, the insurer agrees to make periodic payments to you beginning immediately or at some future date. You can choose to invest your purchase payments in a range of investment options, which are typically tied to the performance of the stock market or a sector of the stock market. The key difference between a regular annuity and a variable annuity is that the value of your account in a variable annuity will vary, depending on the performance of the investment options you have chosen. The main disadvantage to variable annuities is their higher cost. In this regard, you will need to ensure that the benefits you are receiving are commensurate to the fees that you are paying."

"If we could transfer some of our risks to mitigate a potential HIPPie dilemma, we would take a close look at that," said Mary.

"Make it part of your overall portfolio strategy and find the right balance for you," replied Mike.

We left the meeting after agreeing to meet Mike at the baseball stadium later in the evening. Mike was a big baseball fan and wanted us to join him tonight.

17

Insure Your What-If Risks

Mike was waiting for us at Richmond Stadium, in the seats just behind home plate. He had invited us to the Richmond Pirates' last home game of the season. The Richmond Pirates were a Triple A baseball club, located one hour northwest of Oakhill.

"Glad you could make it," Mike said, grinning from ear to ear. "There is nothing like an early evening baseball game to remind me of my days as a youngster growing up in New York."

The smell of popcorn and hotdogs filled the air as Mary and I sat down next to Mike.

"I invited you here a little early, not because I wanted to watch the pregame warm-ups, but because I thought this would be an ideal setting to talk about the importance of protecting against some key financial risks for baby boomers," Mike said as he sipped his soda.

"The Richmond Pirates are first in their division with only an average offense. Any guesses on how they are manufacturing their wins?" quizzed Mike.

"I would have to guess that it's good pitching and good defense," I replied.

"Exactly," Mike said. "The old saying 'A good defense wins championships' is a truism that applies to all team sports. Of course, you need a certain competency in your offensive skills, but there is nothing like great defensive play to win you those extra games and propel you to the top."

"So, protection is about building a good defense?" I asked.

"Yes. What good is it to put a plan together where you know what you want and why, have a system to better capture opportunities, and then get derailed by the first challenge?" Mike replied.

We watched as one of the players cracked a fastball between first and second base. What looked like a sure line drive to center field was quickly gobbled up by a speedy and nimble shortstop. He made a difficult play for most look quite easy as he nonchalantly tossed the ball to the first baseman as part of a warm-up drill.

"Now that's a defensive specialist," chimed Mike as he raised his thumb in the air to acknowledge the skill of the shortstop. "That's someone you want on your team because he can save your game. In your case, a defensive specialist can help you protect and save your retirement."

"That makes sense," Mary replied. "But if defense is so important, then why are we discussing protection at this stage in our conversations?"

"Great question, Mary," replied Mike. "I have been sharing an integrated approach to helping you solve your challenges. I have chosen to explain it in this manner to provide you with chunks of information that you could digest and implement successfully as opposed to being overwhelmed. The truth is that you will be constantly reevaluating your purpose, opportunities, and protection strategies. The more you integrate and coordinate all of your financial affairs and strategies, the more successful you will be."

Over the course of the baseball game, Mike outlined the many risks that could have a substantial impact on the quality of our life in retirement. He reviewed our risks and specific strategies to mitigate those risks. He explained that the main principle behind building a good financial defense was to acquire the most financial protection for the least cost. We then talked specifically about illness and long-term care insurance."

Mike said, "Your first line of defense in relation to not having your plans derailed by a major health event is to take care of yourself. Eating well, exercising, and finding ways to manage your stress are necessary. When I had my heart attack, I learned that more than 60 percent of heart attack victims go on to survive."

"That's good news," I said.

Mike replied, "Yes, it is. But in my case, it took over a year to get back to full strength. I was lucky to have the personal funding in place to take the time to rehab and recoup. You may not be so lucky."

"I see," I replied, thinking about how long we could make it on one salary and the potential derailment of our plans if faced with a similar situation.

Mike said, "It's important to understand that survival rates are improving for the majority of serious illnesses. However, the amount of financial resources required to regain your health, due to escalating health care costs, is also rising. A short-term illness can have long-term consequences for the depletion of your retirement capital."

We watched the remainder of the game focused on the action on the field. It was a great night to watch the defensive team get the better of the challengers and taught us an important lesson in relation to protecting our "what-if" risks.

18

Plan Your Legacy

Mike e-mailed us to meet him at the strangest location I could fathom. As we made our way to the Oakhill Cemetery, Mary and I were not sure what to think. In the distance, we spotted Mike's truck and drove up to it.

"Hello," he said. "A far cry from coffee and pastries."

"Yes," I replied. "We were both surprised by your e-mail instructions to meet here."

"I hope you don't find this too strange," said Mike. "But I come here every so often to be reminded of my own mortality. I come here to think about my legacy. Did I do what I could to make the world a better place while I was here?"

"Isn't it too much of a burden to think one person can make a difference?" I asked.

"In the movie *Pay It Forward*, the character played by Kevin Spacey learns the invaluable lesson of how a random act of kindness can touch multiple lives in a positive manner," Mike said. "I didn't always live this way, but now I can't think of living any other way. Once you get a taste for giving and sharing, you can't go back to scarcity and selfishness."

"My work at the shelter has given me so much more in return than I ever expected," commented Mary.

"I have something I have wanted to share for a while but wasn't ready to until now," Mike said. He took a deep breath and paused as if to collect himself before speaking. "At the peak of my career, my mother had to be moved to a retirement home. I bought her the best that money could buy, but did not visit enough. When she passed away, the guilt spread through every area of my life like a virus. It's one of the reasons I never went back to New York. It's also one of the main reasons I am currently involved with building retirement homes and getting involved in projects that lift my spirit. As Albert Einstein once said, 'Man's greatest purpose is to contribute to the life of his fellow man.' It took me a long time to figure this out, so I have learned not to judge anyone's particular journey."

"We don't have huge amounts of capital to contribute, and we are trying our best to fund our retirement," I said. "What can we do to have a meaningful impact?"

Mike paused and replied, "I hope this doesn't come across too preachy. No matter how bad it gets for us, we have to keep the perspective that we have more than most individuals on the planet."

"That's a sobering thought," I replied.

Mike continued, "When we make the switch from mass consumption to building wealth with purpose, we no longer operate with a flight or fight response. This provides the opportunity to open up and to give and share on many levels that you currently may not be aware of. What you consider a small contribution may be, for the recipient, a lifesaving gift."

"You are right, Mike," I noted. "Just like the experience of walking through the retirement residence with you. The impact you made on those individuals you spent time with cannot be measured in dollars. I know we can easily increase our giving from its current level."

"There are many ways to give," Mike said. "The most obvious is giving time, energy, and financial contributions to worthy causes. Choose to donate to a cause or charity that inspires you. Parents can involve their children in the journey, making it a family affair."

We strolled with Mike through the cemetery. I could not help but think that if this is where we were all going to come to as a final resting place, why did we spend so much time being self-absorbed and selfish? The question of how I want to be remembered was stuck in my mind.

Mike said, "A few years ago, I started to toy with the notion of changing how people define philanthropy. I was inspired by the concept of mass consumption and the way in which western economies flourished when the average citizen gained access to mass-produced goods and services. While many associate the notion of philanthropy with the superaffluent and large family foundations, I believe this is about to change in the coming decade. Most baby boomers will not be in a position to create a personal foundation, but they can make a significant contribution through leaving a lasting legacy. In the case of mass philanthropy, bigger is not necessarily better. Small amounts of capital deployed by a large number of families or individuals can have a significant impact on many social causes around the globe. The driving force behind mass philanthropy is that lasting change can be initiated by a large group of individuals taking effective incremental actions."

I replied, "You are right, and Mary has also been a great example to me. I am going to find something I can get excited about and start contributing my time, energy, and money."

"So, Don," said Mike, "how do you want to be remembered?"

"As someone who cared," I said. "I want my life to mean something beyond my daily survival and my needs and wants. I want to be remembered as someone who cared."

Mike smiled as he put his hand on my shoulder, "We all get to the same conclusion eventually. We are all in this together."

Mike hit us with a final surprise at the end of our meeting. He was preparing to start work on a new and exciting project that would take him away from Oakhill. His wife was joining him on his adventure. The news was both expected and disappointing. But we decided not to dwell on the negative as there were so many positive changes taking place in our lives. We had our own surprise in store for Mike as we set the location for our next meeting.

19

Put It All Together

Within the next two months, we sold and moved out of our house and settled into a condo. By downsizing we gave up some space but gained a number of financial and lifestyle benefits.

"I was a little surprised when you invited me here," Mike said as he strolled toward us. "I have had my eye on this condo development ever since they broke ground."

"I thought you might like to see our new home," Mary replied as she opened the door to the front lobby of the Ivory Towers development and motioned for Mike to continue into the main lobby.

"The place looks great," Mike said.

"We moved in last week and have been enjoying the change immensely. We have taken your advice and executed as best we could. We wanted to share our progress with you today," I said.

"Well, share away," replied Mike.

"By downsizing our home, we have added an extra $180,000 to our retirement savings. Less than what we had budgeted, but as you know, the housing resale market has been pretty tough these days. We were happy to close our deal quickly and take a small loss after commissions. We now own our new condo free and clear of any debt and have paid off all of our credit cards. I can't believe the savings we can generate every month with our debt gone."

"That's fantastic. The savings really start to add up when you pay off your debt," replied Mike.

"In addition," I said, "with my extra travel for my independent contractor opportunity and our desire to keep healthy, we are now much closer to the airport and we have a wonderful health facility in the building."

I invited Mike to join us in our condo. As we entered the elevator to go up to the seventh floor, Mary said, "We are now saving 15 percent of our monthly income and have created a savings account where the money is deposited automatically every month."

Mike replied, "Fantastic. Anything else?"

"After reviewing some real estate opportunities, we decided to buy a two-bedroom condominium in this building. Based on our research, we were able to purchase the condominium and create a net positive cash flow of $400 per month, or a net yield of approximately 5 percent. We believe that we have purchased this property at a good value and also think that the demographics are in our favor."

"How so?" quizzed Mike as we walked out of the elevator and toward the front door of our condo.

"Well, this development is closer to the downtown core than our previous home in the suburbs. It is one block north of the subway and main bus lines. With the growing number of baby boomer offspring demanding flexibility in their careers, affordable housing, and lifestyle alternatives, we believe we are capturing a good opportunity in this demographic," continued Mary.

"I couldn't agree more," confirmed Mike with a large smile, seemingly impressed with our work and logic.

"Please come in," I said, opening the front door of our condo.

"We discovered, through our research, that this investment was better suited for us than the condo across the hall from your investment unit," I said.

"The place looks great," said Mike. "I am impressed not only with the décor but that you had the courage to make the change."

"Come join us coffee and cake," said Mary.

"The real estate investment allows us an opportunity to diversify outside of stocks and bonds," I said. "It's really the first time we have been thinking in terms of strategically allocating our wealth in this way."

"Well done," replied Mike. "As you know, the children of the baby boomers are referred to as Generation Y, and they may be poised to take over the spending mantle from their parents. Born between 1976 and

1994, the oldest member of Generation Y turns thirty-four in 2010. Totaling approximately seventy-six million in number, Generation Y appears to have inherited some of their parents' spending habits. However, demographic differences exist between baby boomers and their kids. In general, Generation Y is more ethnically and racially diverse and have lower incomes than their parents. They are waiting longer to get married and have children. This is a great up and coming market to tap into."

"Yes," Mary replied. "With your help, we have come a long way, and we did it in small steps. Even though we started this process with a lottery mentality, we can both see how important it is to think big and execute in small, measurable steps."

"Exactly," agreed Mike. "And speaking of big ideas with small execution steps, how did things develop with your wealth protection strategies?"

"Well," Mary replied, "with Don being away so much these days, I have had time to research and bring a number of pieces together for us. As you know, we purchased our rental property with a combination of savings and debt. We worked with our accountant to create a corporate structure to hold the rental property and future properties we intend to acquire in the coming years."

"Excellent," replied Mike. "The benefits of tax-deductible debt and proper corporate structuring can be very handsome indeed."

"We have set up a monthly contribution plan to direct most, but not all, of our excess savings into our retirement investments. We have created our strategic asset allocation model to keep us properly invested," continued Mary. "Choosing a conservative portfolio, using ETFs as our core holding, we feel confident that our existing asset allocation will allow us to better weather any financial storms."

"Well done," Mike said. "So now you have a strategic asset allocation strategy, positive rental income, and some good tax breaks from your rental property. You also mentioned that you did not use all of your extra savings. Where did you put the rest?"

"This is the really great part," Mary said. "Combining all of our strategies in an integrated fashion, we were able to allocate a portion of our savings to specific insurance solutions designed to mitigate and transfer some of our financial risks."

"This is what we talked about in relation to using an integrated approach—using one strategy to create multiple benefits," Mike said.

"Right," I replied. "We have gone from zero financial protection to mitigating the bulk of our financial risk. Specifically, we purchased a critical illness insurance policy and a long-term care insurance policy. Both these insurance policies are rather expensive, so as part of our homework we identified key features that were important to us. While we have not fully covered our risks with these two insurance strategies, we are in a much better position today in the event that something does go wrong. As we have discussed in the past, transferring some of our risks is better than have no risk mitigation strategy in place."

"I am often amazed as to how many people who can afford these plans don't take advantage of them," Mike said. "Cost is the biggest deterrent, but you have just proven that by arranging your affairs effectively, you can drastically improve your financial protection."

"With the critical illness coverage and the long-term care coverage, both Don and I feel so much better that our retirement plans will not be derailed by a sudden debilitating illness," Mary said. "The statistics show that recovery rates are improving for most major illnesses, but the financial costs to get better are also going up. We could not afford the huge drain on our resources of not being protected."

"The risk of having some form of major illness, such as a stroke, heart disease, or cancer, increases with age. The idea of trying to fund your recovery or your long-term care costs without proper insurance is frightening," Mike said.

I said, "We are taking much better care of our health, but in the event something did happen, we want to be certain that we are properly protected."

"And we are not done yet," exclaimed Mary.

"Oh really?" chuckled Mike. "What's next?"

"With some of the savings we have accumulated, we were able to purchase universal life insurance policies for both of us," Mary said. "This insurance allows us to protect the value of our estate and transfer wealth to our children on a tax-free basis."

"That's the part that most people simply are not aware of," commented Mike. "Life insurance can be used as an effective investment because of the tax-sheltering capabilities it provides. Properly structured and implemented, it is a powerful tool in your financial protection arsenal."

"Finally, we allocated a portion of our estate to our legacy planning desires. Through our estate, two charities we have identified that we want to support and work with will receive in excess of fifty thousand dollars each," Mary said. "We involved our children in our decision making, and they learned a great deal from this process. In addition, we started to fund various entrepreneurs globally who need microcredit loans. To date, we have helped seven families start a business with less than a thousand-dollar investment. The kids are ecstatic about their involvement in this program."

"Amazing," replied Mike. "I love the fact that you are passing on the legacy of giving to your children. It's truly inspiring."

"Overall, we feel so much better prepared and also feel that we are accomplishing so much more with our wealth," I said with a sigh of relief. "It's the complete opposite of what you referred to as the retirement anxiety trap. We feel as if we are in control of our financial present and future."

"Well, it appears to me that you have made some impressive gains in both your approach and results," Mike said. "But tell me, how are you going to ensure that you are not going to run out of money or capital?"

"The HIPPie dilemma," I replied with a smile. "To mitigate this risk, we have moved a portion of our managed assets to a variable annuity strategy. Variable annuities provide us with a guarantee of capital and a guaranteed lifetime income, regardless of financial market conditions."

"I think that's a great idea," replied Mike. "Variable annuities are fairly new products in the marketplace, but they are designed specifically for those who do want some of the key features of a good pension plan. I think you are going to see more baby boomers gravitate to these types of solutions. Your balanced approach makes more sense than the all or nothing approach advocated by most financial advisors."

"We now have a chunk of our assets in a strategy that provides us with capital preservation and a predictable income stream," I continued.

Mike paused and took a deep breath, as if preparing to say something that we were not ready for, and said, "I am proud of both of you. It takes a lot of courage to make the changes you have put in place. It's one of the main reasons I have continued to share my time and my thoughts with you. You have demonstrated your willingness to listen and make real changes, despite the many obstacles. I do have something important I want to share with you, but would prefer to do it at Café Milano. Come by tomorrow, as I have some important news to share."

- 20-

Stay on Purpose

As Mary and I approached the front door of Café Milano, we were both stunned to see a sold sign hanging prominently in the front window.

"Come in, please," Mike said as he opened the front door. "I can tell by your faces that you are surprised by the sign."

"A little surprised and maybe even shocked," I replied.

"Yes, change is truly the only constant," Mike said grinning. "One of my most loyal customers bought the place last week. She had been after me for more than a year, but I wasn't ready until recently."

"I see," Mary replied, still somewhat confused.

"The individual who purchased the café is twenty-eight years old. She lives a very modest life, with low overhead, and can afford to wait out the tough times ahead. She has a long-term vision for the café and is making some exciting changes to the store in line with her values."

"To be totally honest, there was a time when I wanted to ask you about a franchise opportunity," I said. "But the more I researched the concept, the more I realized that owning a café was not my path."

"Great minds think alike," Mike said, nodding in agreement, "Once you start making decisions based on your purpose and values, instead of simply chasing money, you gain clarity. You have made tremendous progress in this regard."

"So now that you have sold the café, what are your plans for the future?" I inquired awkwardly.

"Well, I have to really thank both of you," Mike said. "Going through this process with you has added a great deal to my life. I didn't see this coming when we first started our chats, but I am ready to move on to the next phase of my life."

"What do you mean?" asked Mary.

"As you were working diligently on your lives, I took the time to revisit my own purpose, values, and goals." replied Mike. "I have come to the conclusion that I have not been true to myself. You inspired me, through the changes you have made, to take a close look at my life and make some changes as well."

"What kind of changes?" Mary pursued.

Mike smiled and said, "I've decided to go ahead with my redevelopment of this block of stores. I just launched a new company called Green Centers Inc., which will develop renewable energy infrastructure for new and existing buildings across the globe."

"That's fantastic," I replied. "I had a funny feeling that the roof-top solar system you installed at Café Milano was only the beginning."

"There is five thousand times more sunlight than we need to meet 100 percent of our energy needs," Mike said. "According to *Kurzweil's Law of Accelerating Returns,* we are approximately twenty years away from a complete shift to renewable energy, harnessing the power of the sun and the wind."

"Very exciting," Mary replied enthusiastically. "Why do most people still view renewable energy as a fringe energy source?"

Mike smiled and replied, "Remember what the pundits said about personal computers, cell phones, and the Internet?"

"All of these technologies were marginalized," I said. "I was part of that group that did not believe that these technologies would accelerate so quickly."

"The renewable energy boom is really a technology boom in disguise," replied Mike. "With increased demand will come increased technological advance, which will drive costs lower and increase demand. It's the virtuous cycle of capitalism."

"With all the doom and gloom out there, the world could use more of your pragmatic optimism," I said.

Mike blushed for the first time in our presence. "I am taking things slowly and being careful not to take too much on at this stage. We are in the early stages of the movement to renewable energy, and many will resist this change. In the long run, we will all benefit from greater use of renewable energies, but getting there is a journey, not an event."

"Do you see green investing as a bright spot?" I asked.

"Yes, Don," replied Mike. "I believe that we are in the very early innings of the renewable energy boom. The boom will be driven partly by the desire to curb C02 emissions globally and partly because individuals across the globe are demanding sustainable energy solutions from their government and industry leaders."

"How do we position some of our investments to participate in this boom?" I asked.

"First, you need to remember the basic rules of investing that we have discussed," replied Mike. "Everything comes back to asset allocation and core and explore. Green investing is more focused on those companies that are creating specific technologies and solutions related to a sustainable environment. They can include companies focused on *wind power, solar power, biofuels, smart-grid,* and *water treatment solutions.* You can use green ETFs for public company exposure or add private opportunities through *limited liability partnerships* and direct investments in infrastructure assets, like the solar installation on Café Milano."

"What are the key benefits of private ownership versus public?" asked Mary.

"Well, the main benefit is that your investment is not subject to the volatility of the stock market," Mike said. "Green ETFs can be even more volatile than the overall stock market. The main disadvantage of private investments is that they are less liquid than ETFs and often require a longer holding period."

"So, green ETFs belong in the explore portion of our portfolio," I said. "And a green energy private investment should be made as part of a long-term income investment."

"Exactly, Don," replied Mike. "As always, the rules of asset allocation and yield must be respected."

"Maybe we should be investing in Green Centers Inc.," I chuckled. "What better investment than to follow Mike Higgins in his new venture?"

Mike laughed and put his hand on my shoulder, "It's not a lottery ticket, but I think Green Centers Inc. will do fairly well during the coming decade. It would be an honor to have you as a shareholder in my new company," smiled Mike.

A Good-Bye and Glimpse into the Future

Before I could say anything else, Mary jumped into the conversation. She had been very curious about Mike's thoughts regarding future trends.

"Speaking of the future," Mary said, "what is your crystal ball predicting as some of the major financial trends for the coming decade?"

Mike paused and replied somberly, "It's an interesting question, Mary, and one I ponder a great deal. The next decade will be very challenging. If massive increase in debt levels has helped fuel excess consumption and growth, then an end to this credit expansion will have the opposite effect. All credit expansions end in the same way: painful deleveraging and deflation. Deleveraging leads to lower assets prices, which in turn creates a negative wealth effect. This in turn leads to lower consumption and lower economic growth. How far can this go? Historical parallels aren't terribly comforting. In Japan, a massive boom in the 1980s was followed by many years of painful deflation and deleveraging. Despite government intervention and a decade of close to 0 percent interest rates, the Japanese stock market is lower today in value than it was twenty years ago. Real estate values have never recovered in Japan to their bubble highs."

"That's a frightening thought," Mary said. "Don't governments know more today about how to fight this deleveraging and deflation?"

"Yes and no," replied Mike. "While governments have more tools and resources to combat deleveraging and deflation, it is my belief that they will underestimate the financial and social forces that are working against them, including the massive impact of an aging baby boomer population. In real terms, individuals own approximately 70 percent of the wealth in North America. Once they decide they need to save more, spend less, and conserve, the government will not be able to counter this powerful force."

"You mean the strain on the financial and social system from the more than ninety million baby boomers entering their retirement years and the fact that the baby boomers realize they need to take greater personal responsibility for their finances?" Mary asked for clarification.

"Exactly," replied Mike. "The problem is that even the majority of governments have been borrowing from the future to fund the present. Remember that every action has an equal and opposite reaction. The baby boomers are waking up to this fact, and you are now witnessing a large increase in personal savings rates and less individual demand for debt. A heavy price will be paid for this shift from debt to savings at all levels of society."

"What price is that?" I asked.

"The government will not be able to borrow at historically low interest rates to fund burgeoning annual financial deficits and debt. You can only borrow from the future for so long without deep consequences, and this borrowing is very close to reaching its limit. The only solutions will be less government spending or increasing taxes. Both of these will act as a drag on future growth. Just like you and Mary have learned to reduce your expenses and increase your savings, the government will be forced to do the same."

"What you're talking about is overspending at all levels of society coming home to roost," I said.

"That's right," replied Mike. "A few years back, politicians used to say that 'government deficits don't matter.' However, after many years of escalating deficits leading to dangerously high levels of national debt, what we have all learned is that deficits do matter. Ongoing deficits led to a ballooning of government debt."

Mary replied, "It goes back to what you said, Mike. Don't count on the government coming to rescue our retirement. Their pattern of overspending and borrowing to fund this overspending is its own mini-bubble that is going to burst as well."

Mike nodded in agreement and said, "Quite right, Mary. The age of unconscious spending and leveraging the future for excessive consumption is rapidly coming to an end. As hard as this will be for many to accept, it is inevitable that a new way of living is upon us. The coming decade of financial upheaval will foster an age of purposeful living and conscious consumerism. Individuals will learn to save more and integrate their pocketbooks with their social values. Governments will learn that they, as well, cannot borrow indefinitely from the future without consequences. Individuals will demand greater stewardship from their elected representatives at all levels. Unfortunately for most, it will take a financial crisis for everyone to wake up and start making changes. But you and Don have learned that you have a choice and that you are responsible for your future."

Mike paused and put his hand on my shoulder. "As you have learned by now, I am not a 'doom and gloomer,' and I don't have an apocalyptic view of our future. Every financial crisis gives birth to the seeds of opportunity. This is the nature of capitalism. Innovation and productivity are the key ingredients for the creation of long-term wealth. I believe that we will see a massive shift to sustainable wealth in the coming decade. The notion that wealth can be created in a manner that also serves the greater societal good is no longer an idealistic view. The desire for a sustainable future, across all levels and facets of society, will be a significant catalyst for job creation and new capital formation."

"It's hard not to be somewhat afraid," Mary said. "But now we know how to deal with our fear in a proactive manner and live by our values. I can say for the first time in our lives, we are living much more in the moment and awake to the choices we are making."

Mike replied, "While the next decade will bring many challenges, those who are prepared will prosper. Consciously choosing the life you want to live and managing your financial affairs, based on your purpose and values, will provide you with the greatest of rewards."

As we said our good-byes, Mike hugged Mary and then shook my hand firmly. "I appreciate our time together and have learned a great deal about myself through your journey. You have been my teachers, and for that I am very grateful. Please stay in touch."

As we exited Café Milano for the last time as a trio, Mike handed me a small laminated card from his shirt pocket. With his trademark smile, he said, "This is a reminder of how far you have come on your journey and that many exciting adventures lie ahead. 'Success is the progressive realization of a worthy ideal.'"

Author Biography

Paul Ghezzi has provided expert financial management advice for more than fifteen years. He is an accomplished speaker and has presented to audiences across North America.

For more information visit www.paulghezzi.com.

www.ingramcontent.com/pod-product-compliance
Lightning Source LLC
Chambersburg PA
CBHW030756180526
45163CB00003B/1052